# A Short Survey of Czech Literature

By

F. CHUDOBA

LONDON

KEGAN PAUL, TRENCH, TRUBNER & CO., LTD.

NEW YORK · E. P. DUTTON & CO.

1924

KRAUS REPRINT CO.
New York
1969

**To the Memory**

OF

**Dr. FRANCIS COUNT LÜTZOW**

*The first Czech Minister to England*
*before Bohemia recovered her independence*

# A SHORT SURVEY OF
# CZECH LITERATURE

LC 25-40

*Reprinted with the permission of the original publisher*
KRAUS REPRINT CO.
A U.S. Division of Kraus-Thomson Organization Limited

Printed in U.S.A.

# PREFATORY NOTE

Towards the end of 1920 I came to London as the first Lecturer on Czechoslovak language and literature at King's College. During the next two years I also delivered three courses of public lectures, arranged by the School of Slavonic Studies : on Czech literature, on the leaders of Czech religious and political thought, and on prominent Czech painters and sculptors. Some of my friends in England conceived the idea to see my lectures in print. At first I hesitated to comply with their wishes, being conscious of my defective style and of the hasty manner in which I had to traverse long centuries and important decades in the cultural development of my nation. Now I venture to publish at least one of my courses of lectures, hoping that as a sort of primer it might be possibly useful to those who would like to get some information of a literature which is hardly known, even by name, in Western Europe. If they find that my English is clumsy, they will not be probably too rigorous in their verdicts, considering that English is not my mother tongue, that I acquired it rather late, and that I learned it more from books than from living men and women. I do not think that this is a sufficient

apology of a writer who *publishes* his volume;
it may, however, excuse his *producing* it under
the pressure of circumstances. My benevolent
advisers will be so good as to take the responsibility of the more deadly sin. I thank them
heartily beforehand.

I am also indebted to Mr. Paul Selver, in
London, who placed at my disposal his translations
and selected from them the illustrative extracts.

BRNO, *22nd January*, 1924.

F. CHUDOBA.

# CONTENTS

## Chapter I

### FROM THE BEGINNINGS TO THE HUSSITE WARS

THE Czechoslovak Republic is a young state, and its name may truly sound rather strange to those who have not yet crossed its frontiers or have not yet looked at a map of the New Europe. But the nation which has founded this state and created its history and literature is considerably older. Long before the Republic there was an independent Kingdom, and before the Kingdom a Principality of Bohemia. And going further back, we cannot pass over in silence the medieval Great Moravian State of Rostislav and his nephew Svatopluk which included besides Moravia and Slovakia, with the northern half of Lower Austria, also a part of Bohemia, anticipating, in some measure, the present Republic. In short, Czechoslovak history is more than a thousand years old, though the term ' Czechoslovak ' has been used, even by the Czechoslovaks themselves, not much longer than a century ; in Western Europe it was practically unknown a very few years ago.

This term means that the Czechoslovak nation consists of two branches : the Czechs, living in

Bohemia, Moravia and a part of Upper Silesia, and the Slovaks, living in Slovakia ; it means that these two branches make one ethnographical and political whole, and that they have only one language, though it exists at present in a double literary form : in the Czech literary dialect and the Slovak literary dialect, the first of which, as a literary language, is much older than the second, in spite of the more archaic appearance of some Slovak sounds and forms. This difference, which is but a slight one and which does not exist at all between the Czechs of Bohemia or Moravia and a smaller portion of the Slovaks, living in the south-eastern part of Moravia, as both of them have always used Czech only as their literary language, is to be explained by the long political separation of the Slovaks in Upper Hungary, the present Slovakia, from their kinsmen in Bohemia and Moravia. They were separated, and for a thousand years subjugated, by the Magyars, a people of the Mongolian race, whose occupation of the lowlands of Hungary, at the end of the ninth century, the Czech historian Palacký calls 'the greatest misfortune that has befallen the Slavonic world for many centuries'. It not only cut off the Czechs from the Slovaks and the Hungarian Slovaks from their Moravian brothers but also detached the Northern and Western Slavs from the southern branch of their race in Lower Hungary and in the Balkans.

The Czechoslovaks belong to the large family of the Slavonic race. They form that part of it which is in direct contact with the Western European nations, and together with the Poles in Poland and the small remnants of the Sorbs or Wends in Upper and Lower Lusatia in Germany, they form the western group of the Slavonic peoples. It is rather difficult to say when they came to Bohemia, Moravia, Silesia and Slovakia from their original home. The medieval Czech annalist Cosmas of Prague, who died in the year 1125, tells us a story of a chieftain called Čech, who, with his people, came from the East to Bohemia which was then quite depopulated. He ascended the solitary mountain Řip between the rivers Ohře and Vltava, saw the beauty and fertility of the country, full of animals, birds, fish and bees, and declared it to be the country which he had promised to his kinsmen and followers. Many Czech chroniclers and historians of later centuries, accepting his story, considered the fifth century or, more precisely the year 451, as a probable date for that event. But the most recent archæological discoveries throw a different light on the pre-historic times of present-day Czechoslovakia.

The tale of Cosmas is possibly not without some truth, but very likely it only furnishes an account of the migration of *one* of the Slavonic tribes that came at some time or other to Bohemia. On the other hand, some recent

discoveries indicate that Bohemia and the neighbouring countries were inhabited long before the
Christian era, not only by diluvial hunters and
later on by various races, partly of Celtic, partly
of unknown, origin, but also by some branch or
branches of the Slavonic race, so that already
several centuries before Christ at least some parts
of Bohemia, Moravia, Silesia and Slovakia were
occupied by the direct ancestors of the present
Czechoslovaks. Centuries elapsed, however,
before the Slavs, strengthened by new and more
numerous tribes of their own race, spread all over
the country, and before the various tribes were
blended into one people which received its name
from the strongest and most warlike of them, the
Czechs, who settled in the centre of Bohemia or
Čechy (as the country is called in their own
language),—in that area where the capital Praha
or Prague arose. It was only then that the real
history of the Czechs began.

The first Slavonic state in the lands of Czechoslovakia was, according to the old medieval
chronicles, that of Samo in the first half of the
seventh century. We know but little of the
origin, character and deeds of this extraordinary
man who, although a Frankish merchant himself,
is said to have united the Slavs of Moravia, Lower
Austria and Bohemia under his sceptre and
defeated, in 624, the Asiatic tribe of the Avars
who occupied the lowlands of Pannonia, i.e., of

Central and North-Western Hungary, from there invading, plundering and devastating the neighbouring countries. Then he founded his own kingdom with Bohemia as its centre, and having defeated also the German king Dagobert, strengthened thereby his position as a ruler of an independent state. But we do not hear anything of his successors, and the next names we find in the oldest chronicles, written by Czech authors, as those of the rulers over Bohemia during the eighth century are more legendary than historical. Yet these semi-historical figures of Krok and his wise daughter Lubuša or Luboša who ruled after the death of her father from the castle of Vyšehrad, and is said to have founded the city of Prague on the opposite bank of the river Vltava ; of Přemysl whom she chose as her husband when he was ploughing his field near the village Stadice ; of Luboša's sisters Kazi and Tetka both of whom were women of unusual gifts ; of the strong Bivoj who, though quite unarmed, caught, overpowered and killed a mighty boar and brought it on his back to the Vyšehrad ; of the war which the Czech Amazons declared against men after the death of their princess—and of many others, do not belong entirely to the dead past, but still live in the memory of the Czech people because they are representatives of its heroic age. Some of the greatest and most national Czech artists, such as

Smetana, Myslbek or Aleš, glorified the princess Luboša or Libuše, as she is now called, in their works as the prophetess of a better future of the Czech nation.

Přemysl the Ploughman founded the oldest Czech dynasty that ruled at first over Bohemia, from the tenth century also over Moravia, and in the second half of the thirteenth century over Austria, Poland and Hungary—up to the year 1306. In that year the last male member of his family, the young king Václav (Venceslas) III, was murdered, probably by a German, at Olomouc then the capital of Moravia. The female line, however, continued, as the sister of the murdered king, Eliška Přemyslovna, married John, the young Duke of Luxembourg, who became King of Bohemia and founded a new royal dynasty.

The first member of the house of Přemysl the Ploughman, whom we know as a quite historical personage, was Prince Bořivoj, the first Christian ruler over Bohemia, the husband of Saint Ludmila and grandfather of Saint Václav or Venceslas, who is the hero of the well-known English carol ' Good King Wenceslas look'd out, on the Feast of Stephen '. It is supposed that both Bořivoj and his wife Ludmila were christened (in the second half of the ninth century) by Bishop Methodius who, with his brother Constantine or Cyril, had founded the Old or Church Slavonic liturgy and literature a short time previously. They were invited from Salonica in 863 by Rostislav, the Prince of Great Moravia, to teach his people, who had already rejected paganism, the true Christian faith in their native language. They did not speak Czech but they spoke the Macedonian dialect of Southern Slavonic which was then more similar to the Czech language than it is now. They translated a considerable part of the Bible into this dialect for which purpose Constantine partly adapted, partly invented a new alphabet, the so-called Glagolitic, which was more suitable to denote the Slavonic sounds than were the Greek or Latin characters. Thus they became the founders of the old Slavonic literature—not only in Moravia and the neighbouring countries but through their disciples also in Bulgaria, Serbia, and Russia. Their work forms an epoc in the spiritual development of those Slavonic countries in which Old or Church Slavonic became not only the liturgical but for some time also the literary language. In Moravia and Bohemia, however, this Church Slavonic period of literature was proportionately of a very short duration, and only a few scanty relics of it have been preserved to the present day. The German priests and bishops unjustly denounced Methodius and his brother as heretics, and when Archbishop Methodius died (885), they endeavoured to get rid of his disciples. They succeeded at last, and

the Slavonic priests and teachers had to escape to
Bulgaria where they found protection at the
court of the great Czar Symeon.

In later centuries the Slavonic liturgy and the
Church Slavonic language were re-established
in two famous monasteries in Bohemia : in the
first half of the eleventh century by Saint
Prokop at Sázava, and in the middle of the
fourteenth century by King Charles in the
Slavonic Monastery at Prague ; but in neither of
these places did Old Slavonic survive more than
six or seven decades. Roughly speaking, we may
say that in Bohemia and Moravia the Slavonic
liturgy, and with it the Church Slavonic language,
were replaced by Latin at the end of the ninth
century. At the same time the Czechs also gave
up the Glagolitic alphabet and began to use
Latin characters, which they have used ever
since—with some modifications, of course, which
were introduced by the reformer John Hus at
the end of the fourteenth century.

For these reasons Old Czech literature does
not begin with Church Slavonic texts but with
two Bohemian chronicles written in Latin, and
with two Czech hymns, only one of which bears
slight marks of the Church Slavonic influence.

The first of the chronicles, called usually
*The Life and Suffering of St. Venceslas and St.
Ludmila, His Grandmother*, was written, accord-
ing to Prof. Pekař, of Prague University, by

CHRISTIAN, a monk of St. Emeran's Monastery at Regensburg in Bavaria at the end of the tenth century. Its author was a son of Prince Boleslav I of Bohemia and a nephew of St. Venceslas. He knew the members of his family as well as the historical background of the violent death of his uncle and great-grandmother, whom he made the heroes of his polished narrative. He therefore could write not only a medieval legend but at the same time the first chronicle composed by a Czech, a small work, but, if we accept the views of Prof. Pekař, also an important historical source, informing us of the oldest period of the Christian Church in Bohemia.

Christian was a cousin of the second bishop of Prague, St. Vojtěch or Adalbert, as he is called in Western Europe, also a Czech martyr who, having been elected Bishop of Prague, had to struggle against the heathen customs of his stubborn countrymen, notably against their polygamy. Twice he left his bishopric and his country; at last he undertook an apostolic journey to Prussia, where he was murdered in the year 997.

The younger chronicle is the greater literary achievement of the two. We know that its author, COSMAS OF PRAGUE, was born about the middle of the eleventh century of a noble Czech family, which gave him a good education at home and abroad; that he extended his intellectual horizon during his several journeys to Germany, Italy and Hungary ; that he married a Czech lady but in spite of this became a priest and later on a canon of the chapter at Prague ; and that after the death of his wife, only a few years before his own death (1125), he wrote his *Chronica Bohemorum*. He relates the story of his country, according to the custom of medieval annalists, from the building of the Tower of Babel, but he is not uncritical. He draws a clear distinction between the old myths and legends which he calls *senum fabulosa narratio*, the tales of old people, and the historical facts, the accounts of which he found in his written sources, in the memory of his elder contemporaries, and in his own political experience. In this respect he surpasses nearly all the contemporary chroniclers in other countries, as well as his Czech successors for the following two or three centuries. His Latin style is elegant. He likes jests and satire, and poetically describes the beauties of his country to which he is closely attached. As a writer and historian he is one of the most interesting figures among the annalists of the Middle Ages.

The oldest Czech hymn, beginning with the words *Hospodine, pomiluj ny* (Lord, have mercy on us), was attributed to the Slavonic missionaries, Constantine and Methodius, or to St. Vojtěch ; other scholars again conclude that it is not quite so old because Cosmas of Prague does not mention its first line when speaking, on a certain occasion, of the Latin and German hymns of a similar type. But being only a version and amplification of the Greek words Κύριε, ἐλέησον, it is beyond all question the oldest Czech hymn we possess, whether it was composed in the ninth, or in the eleventh century. Two or three words in it are Old Slavonic, and therefore it could be only produced when the Old Slavonic liturgy was not yet forgotten in Bohemia. Lastly, also its melody is of a very ancient character and testifies to its antiquity. In the Middle Ages it was sung in churches and on battlefields, and its medieval tune is heard in Czechoslovak churches up to this day.

The second oldest *hymn* is that of *St. Venceslas*, the first verse of which, ' St. Venceslas, duke of the Czech land, our prince, pray for us to God and the Holy Ghost, Kyrie eleison ', characterises it as a fervent prayer of the Czech people to the patron of its country. It seems to have originated at a time of distress, probably in those sad years after the death of the great King Přemysl Otakar II, on the battlefield in Lower Austria (1278), when the Czechs, being oppressed by the foreign government of Otto of Brandenburg, sought consolation in God. Like the older hymn, *Hospodine, pomiluj ny*, it is rhymeless, and it also was sung by Czech soldiers in battle and by the people on solemn occasions in churches and processions. Originally it had three strophes only, but in the later centuries new strophes, to the number of ten, were added, and in these the sentiments and tastes of the time are reflected.

Before John Hus, these two hymns, with two others, were the only ones allowed by the Synod of Prague to be sung in Bohemian churches, all other Czech hymns being prohibited. They were the first harbingers of the Czech literary movement which began in the thirteenth century.

At that time some important changes took place in Bohemia. The first hereditary kings of the House of Přemysl, Přemysl Otakar I, Václav I, Přemysl Otakar II, having consolidated their power at home, were able to strengthen their influence also in the Holy Roman Empire, which was then weakened by internal disputes and struggles. Both they and their brothers married German princesses who introduced the German language and manners into the royal court of Prague. The Czech nobility, imitating their kings, began to adopt German names for their families and castles; the queens, kings, and at least some of the nobles, invited German wandering poets, and what was much worse for the future, also German colonists to Bohemia. Thus they imported a new element into their country, an element which was perhaps not inimical at the beginning, but which became so in later times, when the numbers of these guests increased, and they were prompted by a desire to rule over the country which had invited them.

The Czechs at Prague and in the country were at first quite friendly to them. They exchanged their own simple garb for the richly decorated costumes prevailing in Western Europe and Germany; they adopted West European manners, songs of love and tournaments; and some of them even began to prefer German to their native language. They certainly read the fashionable epic poetry which the Germans imitated or directly translated from French poems of chivalry. And an unknown poet who very likely belonged to the nobility, or at least possessed the social views of a nobleman, went back to the sources and took as his model the popular epic on Alexander the Great, written in Latin hexameters by Gautier de Châtillon, about a hundred years earlier. This he translated, or more properly, re-wrote in Czech rhymed verse as a new *Alexandreis*. Although three-fifths of his work were lost, the fragments which have been preserved are sufficiently good in quality to be placed proportionately high among the literary productions of the end of the thirteenth or the beginning of the fourteenth centuries. His Alexander is a Christian king who fights against the heathen, protects ladies, and is accompanied on his expeditions by princes and dukes, lords and knights, esquires and owners of escutcheons, some of whom have good Czech names and use medieval Czech arms. The author does not care much for classical archæology or historical truth ; he omits nearly all the mythological decorations of his model and overlooks all the discrepancies between the spirit of ancient Greece or Persia and the ideas of his own age. His chief aim is to entertain and instruct his contemporaries in accordance with artistic and moral views of his own.

The Germanophile tendency of the Bohemian kings, nobles and citizens was followed by a reaction, and we find the echo of it not only in contemporary Czech politics but also in literature. The author, known as DALIMIL, the first annalist who wrote a Czech chronicle in Czech verse (at the beginning of the fourteenth century), showed this anti-German feeling in his work very strongly, allowing his own notions and convictions to be expressed through the mouth of Prince Oldřich, who became famous among his subjects and countrymen by marrying the Czech peasant girl, Božena, and not a German princess. ' For everybody's heart ', Dalimil lets him say, ' clings fervently to his own nation ; therefore a German wife will not favour my people. A German wife will have German servants ; she will teach my children German '.

The *Alexandreis* and the *Chronicle of Dalimil* were products of the Czech noble and middle classes as far as these were interested in literature and liberal education. At the same time—and partly at a still earlier date—literature in Bohemia was fostered also by the clergy and the members of several monasteries, the oldest of which was founded at Břevnov, near Prague, in the second half of the tenth century. But the literature which the priests and monks produced was of a different kind. They copied, annotated, and sometimes also translated Latin liturgical books or selected parts of the Bible, and when their skill in Czech versification increased, they imitated, more or less, Latin *legends of the saints* as they found them, especially in the collection of Jacobus de Voragine, known under the name of *Legenda Aurea.* None of these oldest Czech legends : on the Passion of the Lord, on the Apostles, and the Virgin Mary, on Judas or Pilate, have been preserved complete ; but the fragments which we possess testify to a considerable artistic talent on the part of those unknown ecclesiastics who wrote them.

One of these legends, that of Judas, was composed shortly after the violent death of King Venceslas III (1306) as we can see from its allusion to that very important event in the history of Bohemia. Not very long afterwards was produced one of the oldest fragments of Czech dramatic poetry, the so-called *Quacksalver*, a scene showing us, with drastic realism, a picture of medieval life in the form of liturgical drama. A similar realism, but less licentious in character than this primitive and crude play, is typical also of several other productions of the first half of the fourteenth century, first of all the two collections of satires in verse, called *The Decalogue*, and *The Satires on Artisans*, in which an unknown writer castigates the transgressions of his contemporaries, especially their guile and dishonesty. His wit is rather blunt, but his moral consciousness reminds us sometimes of those preachers and moralists who forty or fifty years later prepared the way for Church Reform.

If to this list of the early fruits of Czech literary activity we add several hymns and *historical songs*, the oldest Czech *fable* on 'the fox and the jug', some *didactic poems* and the so-called *Book of Rožmberk* in which an anonymous author for the first time, as far as we know, made a compilation of medieval Czech legal customs for the use of judges and lawyers, we have not enumerated all the works or fragments of works, but certainly nearly all the forms of Czech literature at the end of the thirteenth and the beginning of the fourteenth centuries.

The period which followed the sudden death of King Venceslas III does not belong to the happy ages of Czech history. At first the contests of those who laid claim to the vacant throne of Bohemia, and then the turbulent reign of the spendthrift John of Luxembourg, who was more a soldier than anything else, could not make the country prosperous and happy. The only redeeming feature for which the Czech people gratefully remembers this knight-errant is his glorious death on the battle-field at Crécy in France, where he fought as an ally of the French against the English, to whom he left his three feathers and his device ' Ich dien '. His son, Václav, known in history under the assumed name of Charles IV, was a much better ruler. If we compare the father and son, we do not find many important qualities which they possessed in common. But if we look at Charles's grandfather, King Venceslas II, who died at the age of thirty-four in the year 1305, we cannot help concluding that these two kings of Bohemia were, in some respects, more akin as rulers than any others in Czech history, and that Charles's mother, Eliška Přemyslovna, makes a very significant link between the dynasty of Přemysl and that of Luxembourg. German historians generally describe Venceslas II as a narrow-minded weakling without any prominent abilities. Weaklings, however, do not usually augment their power in such a degree as Venceslas II did. When he ascended the throne of Bohemia (1283) he found his kingdom impoverished by the misrule of his guardian, Otto of Brandenburg; when he died he left it rich and powerful, so that

2

never before, and never afterwards, did the
countries united under the Bohemian sceptre
extend so far as when his young son, Venceslas III
mounted the throne.   And narrow-minded rulers
do not generally concern themselves with estab-
lishing new universities as did Venceslas II, who
was prevented from founding a University at
Prague only by some external circumstances
unfavourable to his plan.   But what he could not
accomplish was done by his grandson, Charles IV
who, in the year 1348, founded at Prague the
first Czech university and at the same time the
oldest university in Central Europe, creating in
this way a new centre of learning and indirectly
preparing the great religious movement of John
Hus and his followers.

He himself was a learned man and writer, a
wise statesman, an unusually practical economist,
and one of the best and most enterprising builders
in the Middle Ages.   The famous stone bridge
in the Old Town, the broad streets and large
squares in the New Town of Prague, the Castle
and the Gothic Cathedral of St. Vitus on the
Hradčany, the strong and beautiful castle of
Karlův Týn to the south-west of Prague, many
Gothic churches and some monasteries both in
the capital and in the country, are lasting witnesses
to his artistic capacity and his prosperous rule.
He also fought bravely, but as Palacký says, ' he
obtained far more by the arts of diplomacy than

he ever could have done by force of arms'.
He was a pious man, who bought and collected
relics of the saints, erected sumptuous chapels
and costly shrines for them, and endowed churches
and monasteries with large estates. Supporting,
however, materially the Church institutions, he
indirectly supported also the luxurious living of
those who declared themselves humble and poor
servants of the Lord. In this respect his efforts
were not progressive, but the final result of them,
which he certainly did not wish but could not
prevent, was a powerful movement against those
institutions that he had endowed so richly. He
did not live to see the first struggles of John Hus
and his friends against the abuses of the Roman
Catholic Church, but he lived long enough to
hear one of Hus's predecessors, Jan Milíč of
Kroměříž, preaching in his presence on the
advent of Antichrist, whom he identified with
King Charles himself.

Thus we see that the epoch of this excellent
ruler, who raised his kingdom to the highest
splendour in arts and sciences, in foreign politics
and home prosperity, was a period of transition.
On the one hand we observe the highest development of the old social tendencies and institutions, on the other, revolutionary currents which
undermine their deepest foundations. On the
one hand a rich priesthood and monasteries
with a very high standard of costly living, on

the other, poor, self-denying apostles of simplicity and love, regarding even the most despised members of human society as their brothers and sisters. And because literature is very often but a mirror of life, we can find these contrasts also in its productions.

Some ecclesiastics, schoolmasters and other unknown writers, who spiritually belonged to the past, produced the same sort of literature as their fathers and grandfathers : *tales and romances in verse* on Tristram and Iseult, on Tandarius and Floribella, on King Laurin and the Garden of Roses ; or *legends* in verse and prose, among which those of St. Catherine and St. Dorothy are the most distinguished from the artistic point of view ; or prosaic translations and imitations of *tales of chivalry*, the heroes of which belonged partly to the Middle Ages, partly to the cycles of stories on Alexander the Great and the War of Troy ; or Latin and Czech *chronicles* in which their authors, Přibík Pulkava of Radenín or Beneš Krabice of Weitmile, followed, not altogether successfully, the example of Cosmas of Prague.

More modern and more realistic are those works in verse or prose which took their subject matter from life of the time. The best and most interesting of them is the satire *The Groom and the Scholar*, in which a country groom and a mendicant student describe in vehement terms the hardships of their lives. A few *lyric songs* of an erotic character belong very likely to the same sphere of student life. The best known of them is the *Song of Záviš*, the author of which studied at Prague in his younger days, and founded what we may call the first school of composers of Czech music.

To this realistic literature we may add some other works which, being traditional in form and tendency, contained at least some germs of the future spiritual development of Bohemia. One of them is the *New Council* by Smil Flaška of Pardubice, an allegorical poem, ending with an emphatic admonition to a virtuous life and a vivid picture of ' that day of wrath, that day of darkness ' on which the awful trumpet will call the sinner to the Last Judgment.

This awful trumpet had sounded in Bohemian churches and also in Czech literature from time to time for about thirty years before Smil Flaška wrote his allegory. The Austrian monk, Conrad Waldhauser, whom King Charles IV had invited to Prague in the sixties of the fourteenth century, and after him especially Jan Milíč of Kroměříž, preached in the Gothic church of Týn at Prague and elsewhere with such success that sinners publicly confessed their sins, fallen women left the houses of ill-fame, rich ladies gave up their trinkets and jewels, and masses of people assembled to hear their vehement attacks on public corruption.

But their powerful eloquence did not influence the wives of rich merchants and the populace of Prague alone. Tomáš (Thomas) of Štítné, the first Czech who composed philosophical and religious prose in the Czech language, confesses how deeply the ' fiery words ' of Milíč affected him and how they inspired him to write his religious tracts and conversations. This country squire, who came as a youth not quite twenty years of age to the new University of Prague and without taking a degree returned to his village in southern Bohemia, was a meditative spirit. The management of his household and family left him time enough both to read Latin books of theology or scholastic philosophy and to reflect not only upon what he read but also upon human life and the relations of man to God. And after his wife had died and his children were growing up he let his estate to a tenant and moved to Prague, where he died at an advanced age, probably in the first year of the fifteenth century.

His chief works are religious and philosophical tracts which he collected in books, called the *Books of General Christian Matters*, then the *Religious Discussions*, and the *Sermons for Sundays and Feast-days*. Besides these he also wrote or translated several minor works. He was not an original thinker in the true sense of the word, for he accepted the scholastic philosophy of Thomas Aquinas and other medieval thinkers, but being a good scholar and a keen observer, he blended the ideas of others with his inner experiences, so that all his utterances are the expression of his harmonious personality.  If we read his clear and terse writings we must wonder how intelligibly and often beautifully he could express in his native tongue even the loftiest ideas of his time.  In this respect he has hardly a rival among the contemporary Western European writers on religion and philosophy.  Some theologians of Prague University were displeased by his using the language of the common people in books on 'higher subjects'.  But Štítný answered their attacks saying that clear water can flow even along foul gutters, and asking them why he should not write in Czech for the Czechs if St. Paul had written in Hebrew for the Hebrews, and in Greek for the Greeks.  For all people were the sons of God and all had an equal right to acquire wisdom in that language which God had given them.

This democratic feature of his views was new and almost revolutionary in the domain of medieval scholasticism.  It foreshadowed the Church Reform of John Hus.

A keener spirit and a more fervent heart in religious efforts, though not a greater writer, was Štítný's younger contemporary MATĚJ (MATTHEW) OF JANOV.  He died about eight years before the squire of Štítné, but at an age that had still many possibilities of further development.  He, too,

was a son of southern Bohemia, that hilly table-
land with pine woods and fish-ponds, and blue
mountains to the South and West, a country which
we could call the cradle of the Czech Reformation;
for Hus, Žižka and Chelčický were also its children.
In his youth he studied at Prague, where he was
strongly influenced by the sermons of Milíč, and
in Paris where he made the acquaintance of some
contemporary criticism of the Pope and the abuses
in the Roman Catholic Church. Afterwards he
returned to Bohemia and spent some time in
poverty, waiting in vain for a prebend. This
circumstance probably strengthened his natural
inclination to reasoning on the corruption in his
church. It resulted in a large collection of Latin
tracts under the common title *Regulæ Veteris
et Novi Testamenti* (Rules of the Old and the New
Testament, 1388-1392) in which he attacked what
we may call the dead formulæ that had killed the
soul of Christianity. He condemns not only the
superficial ceremonies and superfluous church-
festivities, but also the relics, pictures and statues
of the saints, pilgrimages to their shrines, fast-days,
monasteries and convents—in short, all that the
medieval Christian considered a constituent part
of his creed and his Church. His convictions were
so radical that he declared the gallows to be more
useful to a Christian community than the most
devoutly worshipped picture or statue; for the
gallows were an instrument of God's justice,

while the worshipping of pictures and statues was only the beginning of all pagan idolatry. On the other hand he insisted that knowledge of the Bible was the main source of true Christian theology and a code of Christian morals. He liked neither scholastic philosophy nor the arts as ornaments or accessories of religion. His idea of religious life is as unadorned and austere as a chapel of the Calvinists who came two hundred years after him.

It is quite natural that the Roman Catholic Church did not approve of such books as his and that its authorities at Prague ordered him to revoke the teaching, contained in some works of his, written before his ' Rules '. Later on they asked him to submit for inspection two Czech books which have since been lost. We do not know whether he complied with their request on the second occasion, but we know that he did comply with their order in the first case. He was dismissed with a light punishment although he did not recant in his own heart as we can see from his great Latin work which he produced later. In all probability he was not a man of that strong character which is the most prominent feature of JAN (JOHN) HUS.

The extant accounts of the youth of this reformer and martyr are rather scanty. We only know that he was born in the village of Husinec in southern Bohemia about the year 1370 ; that he studied at Prague where he became a Bachelor

and three years afterwards a Master of Arts ; that
he lectured at the University ; that he took a
degree of Bachelor of Divinity, and that about the
year 1400 he was ordained a priest.  As he himself tells us, this event was a great turning point
in his life.  Up to his ordination he did not live
differently from other young students and
graduates at that time ; he was fond of elegant
attire, and good meals, merry entertainments, and
the game of chess.  But after having been
ordained, he changed his way of life, accom-
modating his personal views and tastes to the high
aim of reforming the Church which had lost so
much of its earlier simplicity and Christian
humility.  The books and tracts of Wyclif which
Czech students had brought from Oxford gave
him an impulse towards a keener criticism of the
Church both ' in head and limbs '—a criticism
which he continued in his sermons at the
so-called Bethlehem Chapel in Prague where he
was appointed preacher in the Czech language
(1402).  From that time onwards his popularity
spread in the Czech nation very rapidly, so that
later, when the Church authorities, who supported him at the beginning of his public career,
prohibited him from preaching at the Bethlehem
Chapel and at last excommunicated him, he went
to southern Bohemia and preached to large
crowds of peasants in the fields and meadows.
And it was as if the strength of ten thousand

hearts that beat towards him, and the enthusiasm of ten thousand eyes that were fastened upon him, entered his soul, and encouraged him to go to Constance, where the General Council of the Church assembled, in order to defend his cause which he believed to be just. Although he had received a letter of safe conduct from King Sigismund he was arrested shortly after his arrival at Constance, and imprisoned in a dark dungeon. They summoned him to revoke all the articles which were declared heretical and, rightly or wrongly, were attributed to him. He was, however, not allowed to defend himself by arguments, to defend the freedom of conscience, though they allowed him *pro forma* to appear before the Council. 'When he attempted to speak', wrote a witness of this official hearing, 'he was interrupted, and when he was silent, the cry arose, " He has admitted his guilt " '. His cause was decided before the first word of his defence was pronounced. Accordingly, on the sixth of July, 1415, they took him out of the city of Constance, burnt him as a heretic and scattered his ashes on the Rhine. Ten months after him the same fate befell also his friend and countryman, Jerome of Prague.

The greatness of Hus is founded not so much on the originality of his ideas or the profundity of his thoughts, as on the strength of his character. He would be a great man even if he were not an eminent writer, or even if we agreed with the sentence passed by the Council of Constance. His was not a stubborn nature. His eloquent sermons which he collected in his largest Czech work, entitled *Postilla,* his numerous Czech and Latin tracts, and, above all, the letters he wrote from prison to his friends in Bohemia, show him to be a tender-hearted man who dearly loved those poor priests and scholars at home, who thought of their needs even in the last hours of his life and was concerned about their spiritual and bodily welfare when he himself was deprived of the commonest necessities of life. He was no fanatic, no zealot. The strength of his character seems to be as natural as his literary style, as his language which he took, we may say, out of the mouths of the Czech people, of those craftsmen and peasants who assembled at the Bethlehem Chapel in Prague or under the tall lime trees in southern Bohemia in order to hear him speak both of the loftier subjects and of those which lay quite near to their hearts and simple minds. They knew that he was one of them and that he understood their thoughts and feelings, and they therefore loved their Master John, and when the news of his execution reached Prague and spread all over the country, their simple, honest hearts were seized by such a feeling of anger that it took twenty years before the flames of this spiritual conflagration were quenched—not by the General

Councils of Constance and Bâle, not by the crusades of German kings and Roman Cardinals, but only by the law of nature which imposes limits even upon the deepest feelings and the most vehement actions.

When, however, the last battle of the Hussite wars was ended and the last fighter of God had perished, a new religious spirit arose out of their ashes, a spirit of forgiveness, of reconciliation, of a new love for mankind.

# Chapter II

## THE HUSSITES AND BRETHREN

The time of the Hussite wars in the first half of the fifteenth century was a period both of deep religious feeling and of national self-consciousness. If the Pope and the Council of Constance believed that they could curb the Czechs by executing their spiritual leaders or by menaces and military invasions, a short experience demonstrated quite clearly that they were greatly mistaken. The Czechs not only refused to obey their commands but on the contrary they became more obstinately attached to their new doctrines and more energetic in carrying through their practical consequences. They expelled the priests who opposed the views of John Hus, appointed his adherents instead of them, and seized by force the estates of the Bishop who belonged to the most fierce enemies of the martyr of Constance. In some respects they were more radical than Hus himself. Six months before his death one of his friends, Jakoubek (or Jacobellus) of Stříbro, a magister of the University of Prague, introduced a new practice which afterwards became very important in the development of the religious and political

movement of the Hussites. He not only began
to preach that the sacrament should be received
in both kinds also by laymen, but he actually
dispensed the communion in some churches at
Prague according to his doctrine, creating in this
way the religious, and in consequence also the
political, party of the Utraquists. This innovation spread apace, and in a short time the chalice
became the chief emblem of all who were enthusiastic in supporting the Reform of the Church in
Bohemia.

But very soon a more radical party arose
among the Utraquists. These radicals declared
the Bible the only source of religious knowledge,
the only authority in religious matters. They
rejected mass and all the sacraments with the
exception of baptism and holy communion, they
set aside the Roman Catholic doctrine of purgatory, the vestments and nearly all ceremonies.
As the city of Prague and particularly the University became the centre of the more moderate
Utraquists, the adherents of the new party, to
which especially the peasants and the lower
classes belonged, founded new centres in the
country districts, often giving them Biblical names,
such as Zion, Tabor, Horeb, Jordan, Josaphat or
Mount of Olives. The most important among
them was Tábor, a town which was founded in the
year 1420 in southern Bohemia, near the small
town Ústí which has since disappeared. It

increased very quickly and became a rival of
Prague, when the party which claimed it as its
headquarters found their leader in the person of
Žižka, the famous warrior.

This man also was born in the south of
Bohemia. His father was a squire at Trocnov,
he himself spent some years at the court of King
Venceslas IV in Prague, probably as a page to
Queen Sophia. At that time he possessed only
one eye, having lost the other in some skirmish
in his youth. Later he lost also the other eye;
but his intellectual power and intuition remained
undiminished, so that he was never defeated,
though he had to fight against enemies who were
much more numerous and much better equipped
than his troops of peasants, artisans and farm
labourers. As these had no armour to protect
them from the German knights, he created new
tactics. The light infantry, equipped with short
spears and shields, or with flails and clubs studded
with iron nails, became the main body of his
army; wagons, protected by iron plates and
linked together by iron chains, became his forts,
and small cannons, introduced only a short time
before, his chief weapon of defence and attack.
Moreover, better than anyone else in his time and
country, he knew how to accommodate his
tactics to the configuration of the ground.

All these circumstances, however, would not
explain satisfactorily his victories over the armies

of King Sigismund if we forgot the religious enthusiasm of his troops and the discipline which was one of its results. Žižka's ' Regulations of a War ', issued in the year 1423, show us the spirit which governed these 'warriors of God'. They had an absolute confidence in God, they identified their cause with God's, and therefore acted as if they were a tool in the hands of God. They abolished all social distinctions among themselves, being only brothers and sisters ; but at the same time they punished by death and confiscation of property everyone who left their ranks, because such a man as steals away from the cause of God and his true brethren was, as they said, like ' an infidel thief '. Their religion was not always that of love, and resembled sometimes more the spirit of the Old Testament than that of the Gospel of Jesus. Though they were not so cruel as they were alleged to be by their adversaries—and above all Žižka himself had very human sides to his character—we cannot deny that their hatred of the infidel and their rigour in punishing the ' deadly sins ' resulted sometimes in fanaticism.

For this reason they were criticised rather harshly both by the Papists and by those whose Christianity was not so austere. The greatest of these latter critics is PETR CHELČICKÝ.

We know but very little of this remarkable man. His name is derived from the village

Chelčice in southern Bohemia where he was probably born about the year 1390, and where he certainly lived in his later years as a farmer. In his youth he went to Prague but because he did not speak Latin, the University remained closed to him. It is, however, probable that he became personally acquainted with John Hus before his exile and that he was strongly influenced by his works and personality. Hus and his friends might have explained to him the contents of the Latin works of Wyclif, Matthew of Janov and other reformers, but he himself used his critical intellect on this body of doctrine. When at the end of the year 1419 the Taborites asked the Doctors and Masters of Prague University whether it was allowed to defend the truth of Christ with a sword and the Doctors and Masters wavered in their reply, Chelčický declared emphatically that no true Christian could consider this to be permissible. He condemned all bloodshed and was so consistent in his views that he left Prague in the following year because Žižka and his followers could not defend their freedom otherwise than by shedding blood in the battle of Vyšehrad (1420) in which they defeated the army of King Sigismund. After this battle he returned to his village in southern Bohemia and there spent the rest of his life. He died about the year 1460.

In his seclusion he reflected on Christianity and the ways in which the contemporary world

was proceeding to carry out Christ's command-
ments. The results of his meditations may be
found in his tracts and two larger works, all of
which he wrote in Czech. The more voluminous
of his books is called *Postilla, or a Book of Interpretations of the Gospel for the Whole Year ;* the
smaller one bears the title *Net of the True Faith.*
This title is more than symbolical. It indicates
the subject-matter of Chelčický's reasoning
which is contained in some verses of the fifth
chapter of St. Luke's Gospel, where Jesus says to
Simon Peter on the lake of Gennesaret : ' Launch
out into the deep, and let down your nets for a
draught. And Simon answering, said unto him,
Master, we have toiled all the night, and have
taken nothing ; nevertheless at thy word I will
let down the net. And when they had this done
they inclosed a great multitude of fishes : and
their net brake ' (St. Luke v. 4-6). Referring to
this scene, Chelčický shows in the first part of
his book how the net of the true Christian faith
was broken by two big whales : the Roman
Emperor Constantine and the Pope Sylvester,
who turned the Christian creed of poor and
humble people into a state religion and thereby
infused poison into the veins of the Church.
For they established two secular laws, two
institutions : the institution of a Christian State
and that of an un-Christian Pope, whereby the
state of Christianity, as he says, was diminished and

fell into decay. These two institutions produced then the most harmful disturbances in the Christian world and at last the death of the Christian faith and of the law of God.

This he tries to prove in the second part of his book, demonstrating in it how the *roty*, i.e., the various classes of Christian Society, such as the nobles, the townsmen, the clergy and the learned men, have increased in number and power in consequence of the worldliness of the Church, what harm they wrought by their un-Christian practices, and how they at last became a great obstacle to the knowledge of the true Gospel of Jesus. The priests raised themselves above other classes, making themselves mediators between the Christians and Christ, and compelling the Christians to obey them rather than God ; they changed piety, the fervent love of God, into a mechanical fulfilling of their own ecclesiastical precepts and into a performance of superficial ceremonies. The property which the Church acquired, destroyed the apostolic poverty and humility, the pagan wisdom corrupted the original purity and sincerity of Christian minds. The learned theologians added unnecessary and ignoble devices to the Christian creed, such as purgatory, indulgences, the worshipping of pictures and statues, forgetting that the true faith could be only a gift of the Holy Ghost and not the result of learning.

A true Christian who wishes to live according to the Bible cannot take part in the governing of the State because the State is a pagan institution, and the acknowledgment of the State by the Church has not rendered it more Christian. No one has the right to compel other people by force to do good, not even the State. If all people lived in accordance with the law of God, no State would be necessary; the existing circumstances make it necessary, but no true Christian will prolong its existence by supporting it as a state official, soldier or priest of the established Church. His only place is among those who earn their daily bread by their own work as peasants, workmen or artisans, who maintain not only themselves but also the ruling classes, though the latter inflict upon them penalties, punishments and other sufferings. He will not repay them with evil for evil, but only with good. And especially under no circumstances will he serve as a soldier in any army whatever, remembering that the strict commandment of God says : ' Thou shalt not kill ' ! No wars, no capital punishment can be allowed in a Christian community because they are the tools of vengeance, and vengeance is God's alone. On the contrary, a true Christian always keeps in his mind the commandment of Jesus ; ' But I say unto you, That ye resist not evil '—and also acts on it as a true son of God.

This perfect unselfishness and readiness for sacrifice is, in Chelčický's view, much more urgent than a distant ideal. He feels that this is the law which necessarily governs the life of true Christian Society. He acknowledges no difference between races, nations and social classes, between rich and poor, being convinced that all men should be brothers, with equal rights and equal duties. He does not consider his views to be the romantic illusion of a dreamer who overlooks reality ; he does not perceive human weakness, but sets before the eyes of his contemporaries a millennium, and strictly orders them to direct their steps towards it. In this respect he is one of the most radical moralists in the Middle Ages and a direct predecessor of Tolstoy, who was astonished to find from a Russian translation of *The Net of the True Faith* that this Czech peasant had preached to his obstinate countrymen the same ideas which he himself disseminated in Russia four hundred and fifty years after him.

Both of them had their followers : Tolstoy, rather unhappily for Russia, in those members of the intelligentsia who, during the war, wishing to be consistent, directly and indirectly helped to dissolve the Russian army and state ; Chelčický, in a circle of craftsmen and peasants who gathered round him in his village and accordingly received the name of the ' Brethren of Chelčice '. Another small community of his adherents was at first protected by the Archbishop of the Utraquists, Jan Rokycana, who recommended his hearers to read the books and tracts of Chelčický, although he did not agree with him in some theological questions. But afterwards, when the danger arose that a new religious sect would augment the difficulties of the Hussite king, George Poděbrad, Rokycana asked the king to give them some land in a remote estate of his in north-eastern Bohemia. He hoped that they would mingle with their neighbours and so disappear as an independent body. They, however, increased in numbers and intensified their discipline. Under the leadership of Brother Řehoř, who was a relative of Archbishop Rokycana, they broke with the Utraquists, elected their own priests and an elder or bishop (1467), and before the end of the fifteenth century their small community spread not only all over Bohemia but also in Moravia, founding their churches in various towns and holding meetings in their own buildings.

For some time only poor and mostly un-learned men and women formed this new religious sect of the Bohemian Brethren. They believed with their spiritual father Chelčický that only those who were poor and simple could observe the true Christian creed. But soon they felt their isolation, and therefore tried to get into touch with other Christian Churches of pure doctrine and uncorrupted life, seeking them in far off countries. We possess a description of the travels of Brother Martin Kabátník, who, towards the end of the fifteenth century, was sent to Palestine, Syria and Egypt to see whether there existed the supposed original apostolic Church. He did not find it, nor did any of the other Brethren who had travelled to Eastern and Southern Europe. And as their own Church had to defend its doctrines against learned adversaries, those Brethren who were not narrow-minded, perceived the importance of a higher education, and endeavoured to win over the majority in their Church. After some struggles with the more conservative or the so-called 'small party' they succeeded. This change in the inner organisation of the Unity of the Bohemian and Moravian Brethren was of vital importance not only for the development of their Church but also for Czech literature and culture. From that time the Unity became the chief centre of all higher efforts in the Czech nation. In the second half of the sixteenth century it possessed the best elementary and secondary schools, the best discipline, the best models of the Czech language, and produced many of the best works in literature. It combined Christian piety with the love of knowledge, and a humble 'brother' could be at the same time a learned humanist.

But, of course, Czech literature of this period

could not develop so richly as the contemporary literature in Italy, France and England. The soul of the Czech nation was seized by a religious passion and remained under its powerful influence too long to be able to produce works of a similar kind to those we find in Western Europe during the Renaissance. From the end of the fourteenth to the middle of the seventeenth centuries, Bohemia resembled England at the time of the Civil War and the Commonwealth. The horizon was never entirely free from threatening clouds, so that the soul of the nation did not find leisure enough to produce lyric songs, dramas and epics of chivalry or dreamland. The only poetry she could produce, and partly did produce, was the religious hymn or the religious allegory. But she brought forth no Milton. For we cannot think of Milton without thinking of his great predecessors, Spenser and Shakespeare. In Bohemia, however, no Spensers, no Shakespeares were possible during the Hussite wars and those six or seven decades which followed them. And when it seemed—at the end of the sixteenth century—that the Czech people had begun to develop new poetic power, another dark cloud appeared in the western sky and a terrible religious storm destroyed all hopes. Rome had been watching Bohemia ever since the days of the Council of Constance, waiting for an opportunity to settle accounts with her.

Therefore almost the whole of Czech literature of the fifteenth, sixteenth and seventeenth centuries was written in prose. As instruction or morals concerned it much more than the fruits of imagination or beauty of form, the general reader of to-day does not return very often to its volumes of theological tracts and collections of sermons, of political or ecclesiastical histories, of cosmographies and codes of law, of grammars and memoirs ; and he is usually not attracted even by the poems of Czech humanists because they are composed in Latin, and being mostly lacking in originality both of ideas and expression, they do not appeal to his modern taste.

But there are some books which are still worth reading and which for this reason have been reprinted during the last hundred years. Such are for instance some descriptions of travels to western and eastern countries. The short book of Martin Kabátník has been already mentioned. More valuable than his are some other accounts of travels and pilgrimages undertaken during the fifteenth and sixteenth centuries partly to Palestine, Egypt and Constantinople, partly to Germany, France, Switzerland, the Netherlands, England, Spain, and Italy. One of them describes the experiences of the retinue of Lord Kostka of Postupice, who was sent in 1464 by King George Poděbrad to France to negotiate with King Louis XI ; another, of about the same time, gives

us a report of the strange adventures of Lord Lev
of Rožmitál and his suite in Western and Southern
Europe. Others again tell of journeys and
voyages to Venice, Dalmatia, the Mediterranean
and the Holy Sepulchre in Jerusalem. The
greatest merit, however, among all these descriptions is exhibited by the *Adventures of Václav
Vratislav of Mitrovice*, a Czech nobleman who in
his youth joined the imperial ambassador to
Constantinople and after his return to Bohemia
wrote a memoir of the misfortunes he and his
comrades endured among the subjects of the
Sultan : how they were arrested by the Turks
who disregarded the rules of international law ;
how they were sent at first to the arsenal and the
galleys, where they had to work like slaves, and
then to a dark dungeon ; how they suffered from
hunger and filth for two years, until some victories
of the imperial army and a rich ransom brought
about their release from that ' grave of the living '.
His simple, but pleasant and touching narrative
remained unpublished for nearly two hundred
years. When it was printed (in the last quarter
of the eighteenth century) it found many grateful
readers and was translated into several languages,
both for its interesting contents and for the charm
of its unaffected style.

Similar in its character is another contemporary memoir of suffering, the so-called *Life of
Jan Augusta*. Its author, JAKUB BÍLEK, was a

priest and a member of the Unity of the Bohemian
Brethren. During a persecution of the Unity by
Ferdinand I, the first King of Bohemia belonging
to the Habsburg dynasty, he was arrested, and
together with the bishop of the Unity, Brother
Jan Augusta, was imprisoned at Prague and
afterwards in the castle of Křivoklát. There
they spent sixteen years, until the wife of Arch-
duke Ferdinand, Philippa Welser, who visited
them in their dungeon and saw their condition,
induced her husband to set them free. Bílek
began to write his story of the woeful experiences
of Bishop Augusta in prison, and finished it after
his deliverance, but it was never printed during his
lifetime. Thus, one of the most impressive
narratives of older Czech literature found its way
to the hearts of the readers as late as in the first
half of the nineteenth century.

These books depict rather the private lives
of more or less important personages than the
public affairs of those times. But we also possess
some memoirs and chronicles of the sixteenth
century which throw light on the life of large
communities and to a certain extent on the life
of the whole nation. Two at least have to be
mentioned, at any rate, if only by name : *The
Chronicle of Prague*, by BARTOŠ PÍSAŘ, and *The
Acts or Memoirs of the Troubled Years* 1546 *and*
1547, by SIXT OF OTTERSDORF. Bartoš Písař was
only a linen-draper at Prague, but being talented

by nature and having access to the documents
he produced one of the most interesting pictures
of public life at Prague in the years 1524-1527.
His younger contemporary, Sixt of Ottersdorf,
was also a citizen of Prague.   But having received
a higher education at home and abroad, he
became a town clerk and afterwards the chancellor
of that city.   During his chancellorship a struggle
broke out between King Ferdinand I and the
Estates of Bohemia whose privileges the King
had endeavoured to curtail.   He succeeded only
partially, but vented his anger on the towns,
and notably Prague.   Sixt was dismissed from his
office and imprisoned for having bravely defended
the freedom of the city.   After he had been
released, he wrote a history of this struggle and
a defence of the cause of the Estates.   He could
not be quite impartial, being himself engaged
in the affairs he describes, nevertheless he contributed materially to our better knowledge of
those times.

As regards Czech history of this period, and
especially its sources, the greatest credit is due
to the Unity of the Bohemian Brethren.   Com-
pelled by the unique position which they occupied
among the Bohemian Churches, to defend their
doctrines against their adversaries, they very early
realised the value of legal and other documents
and began to collect them.   In the year 1546 their
*Archives* were destroyed by fire, but they started

afresh with their efforts, and during the second half of the sixteenth century, they managed to collect, to compile or to compose fourteen big folio volumes of important documents and historical records. They preserved them secretly in various places in Bohemia and Moravia, and when they had to leave their country, they took them to the Polish town Lešno, where they found a new home. These records were discovered there in the nineteenth century and are now preserved for the most part in the present centre of the Moravian Brethren, at Herrnhut in Saxony.

This is the first of their great collective literary achievements. The second one is their classical translation of the Bible. The Czechs possessed a complete translation of the Scriptures before John Wyclif and his collaborators translated it into English. This medieval translation was often copied, several times corrected, and from the latter part of the fifteenth century it appeared in print. As it was made, however, not directly from the original texts but from the Latin Vulgate, and, moreover, as many expressions in it were obsolete, the Brethren undertook the task of translating the Scriptures anew from the Hebrew and Greek originals. Their bishop, JAN BLAHOSLAV (1523-1571), a Moravian by birth, one of their best scholars and an eminent writer on history, language and music, translated the New Testament from the Greek and

published it in the year 1564. After his premature
death a group of nine scholars, belonging to the
Unity, translated the Old Testament from the
Hebrew and printed it, together with a new
edition of his translation, in six annotated
volumes at their secret printing press in the
Moravian village of Kralice. This *Bible of
Kralice*, as it is usually called, is one of the standard
works of older Czech literature. Its language is
not only correct and fluent, but also beautiful
in its simplicity and terseness. In this respect it
greatly surpasses the elegant but highly artificial
and latinised language of the contemporary
historian and lexicographer, DANIEL ADAM OF
VELESLAVÍN (died 1599), and his followers whose
works were considered models of perfect Czech
style for more than two centuries and caused some
uncritical writers in later times to call the period
of Veleslavín the Golden Age of Czech literature.
When this illusion vanished, it was the Bible of
Kralice which influenced the best Czech authors,
especially at the time of the National Revival
when they had to learn from older books how to
use their mother tongue correctly because they
could not learn it either in the Germanised
schools, or in the Germanised society.

It is perhaps not too much to suppose that if
the development of Czech literature had not been
interrupted by a new religious war, this pure and
perfect language of the Bible would, in the hands

of a talented poet, have become something more than excellent prose. In some works of Komenský, e.g., in his *Labyrinth of the World*, we see the first glimpses of this poetic power which, if it had been more developed, might have created works of a different and higher artistic type than the religious thinkers and polemists, historians and orators, compilers of dictionaries and grammars were able to produce. There were authors during the sixteenth century who made Czech verses ; there were pious men who infused their religious feelings or doctrines into hymns which were afterwards collected and published in large folio volumes for the use of the Church. But none of them was a true poet. There were also numerous Czech humanists who wrote elegant hexameters and pentameters, and at least one of them, BOHUSLAV HASIŠTEJNSKÝ OF LOBKOVICE (†1512), outstripped the erudite imitators of Virgil or Horace. But their Latin odes, eclogues, elegies, and satires did not generally survive their authors. On the whole we find more real poetic emotions in some parts of the contemporary prose works than in the versified productions of those rationalistic scholars. And when it seemed that the soil had lain fallow long enough to yield a better harvest, the storm of a new religious war arose.

In 1618 the Thirty Years' War broke out. It began at Prague with the defenestration of two chief councillors of King Ferdinand II by the

exasperated Protestant nobles who were not
willing to endure any longer the oppression of
their Church. Two years afterwards they were
defeated in the one-hour battle of the White
Mountain by the Roman Catholic army of
Ferdinand and the Catholic ' Liga '. This time
the Czech people, the peasants and labourers,
were not much interested in the affairs of their
nobility, having been deprived of their rights
and freedom by the lords in the year 1500.
Therefore when the mercenary army of the
Bohemian Estates was overthrown and dispersed,
the nobles had no other support, and were obliged
to surrender to the king or to escape into foreign
countries. Twenty-seven of the leaders were,
however, caught and beheaded on the Old Town
Square in Prague, on the 21st June, 1621.
Ferdinand was not gracious to the rest. Some of
the ' rebels ' were imprisoned, others deprived of
their property, others again left their country
never to return, knowing what fate would befall
them at home. The chief aim of the victorious
king, who himself was educated by the Jesuits,
was to re-establish the Roman Catholic Church
in a country that was almost entirely Protestant.
He succeeded with the help of the Jesuits in
compelling the inhabitants of Bohemia and
Moravia to confess publicly the new creed though
they did not renounce their own religion in their
hearts. The peasants, who were not free, had to

remain in the country which during the long war was devastated and depopulated to about one third of its former number of inhabitants. The citizens and nobles who were not declared guilty of the rebellion were allowed to sell their estates, if they could, and go abroad. The estates of those, who had escaped or who were found guilty, were simply confiscated and given for nothing or nearly nothing to the adventurers from all quarters of Europe who served the Roman Catholic cause. Many thousands of noble and other families went to Saxony, Brandenburg, Poland, Hungary, Holland, or wherever they found a refuge, hoping that they would be able, sooner or later, to return and take possession of their property they had to abandon. Many of them entered the Protestant armies in Germany in order to fight against their common enemy. Others again served the Protestant cause in other ways. But all of them were disappointed. When the Peace of Westphalia was concluded (1648), none of them was allowed to return to Bohemia or Moravia because Ferdinand III declared that he and the Roman Catholic Liga would rather continue the war indefinitely than allow even one Protestant to live in these two countries. Thus the Czech people lost its nobility, its best citizens, its independence. The greatest part of its territory became the property of foreigners who spoke foreign languages and subscribed to an unsympathetic creed, who

neglected the education of the subjugated people,
or when they did turn their attention to it, tried
to eradicate all national feeling in schools and
churches.

With the educated classes Czech literature also
had to migrate to Poland and Germany. At home
there was no place for those whose character was
not pliable enough to accommodate itself to the
new order of things, established by Ferdinand II.
Two Czech authors were executed on the Old
Town Square: KRYŠTOF HARANT OF POLŽICE
who had produced an elaborate description of
his pilgrimage to Venice, the Holy Land and
Egypt (1608), and VÁCLAV BUDOVEC OF BUDOV
whose *Anti-Alkoran* compared Mohammedanism
with Christianity and advocated concord to
the Christian Churches in the face of their
common enemy. Others left Bohemia or
Moravia before they were arrested and beheaded,
or at least imprisoned. Some, such as the
eminent political writer, KAREL THE ELDER OF
ŽEROTÍN, went abroad willingly, sharing the fate
of their compatriots. Only a few Roman
Catholic writers remained at home and for some
time kept Czech literature precariously alive.

Among those whose destiny it was to die in
foreign countries were two important historians:
PAVEL SKÁLA OF ZHOŘ who in his exile composed
the largest historical work ever written by a
Czech, a *History of the Church*, in which he dealt,

however, also with the political development
of Europe and, above all, of his own country. He
died in Saxony some time after 1640 and left his
ten enormous volumes in manuscript. His
contemporary, PAVEL STRÁNSKÝ, found his second
home in Poland, where he wrote, besides other
books, a Latin work entitled *Respublica Bojema,*
a scientific description of the Bohemian State
before the battle of the White Mountain. He
was happier than Skála, as he was able to publish
it in Holland himself.

Greater than any of them as a man and writer
was JAN AMOS KOMENSKÝ (Comenius), the last
Bishop of the Unity of the Bohemian Brethren.
He was a Moravian by birth, and his native
country gave him his first education. Then he
studied, for about two years, at the universities
of Herborn and Heidelberg, completing his
education by travelling through Holland and
Germany. On his return home he became a
teacher in the same school at Přerov where he
had been educated. Afterwards, having been
ordained, he was sent as a preacher to the most
eastern part of Moravia. In the little town of
Fulnek he married, and spent, perhaps, the
most pleasant time of his whole life. This
period of happiness did not last long. In the
year 1621 a troop of Spanish soldiers who, after
the battle of the White Mountain, had been
scouring the country, burning towns and villages

and killing the Brethren wherever they found them, compelled him to leave his property, his books and manuscripts, and flee to other parts of Moravia and later to eastern Bohemia. There, together with some other preachers of the Unity, he found refuge in one of the estates of the Lord of Žerotín, who himself was a Brother. His wife and children died from the plague, and there were other sufferings which added to his general distress. Under these circumstances he wrote several pamphlets of a meditative and religious character and his *Labyrinth of the World and Paradise of the Heart*, an allegorical poem in prose, telling how all worldly efforts are futile and worthless and how the only spot where a Christian can find rest and happiness is in the recesses of his own heart if he trusts God. But the value of this book (which has been translated into several languages, including English) lies not so much in its moral teaching as in the astonishing abundance of keen observation of contemporary society, and in its terse and racy language. Although he later produced much more than one hundred other works, he never wrote a book which was more perfect from the artistic point of view, and more fresh and spontaneous than his *Labyrinth*.

In the year 1628 Komenský had to leave Bohemia for ever. He wandered from country to country, from district to district, seeking help for his unfortunate country and trying to

bring its cause to the notice of influential persons.
The first years of his sad pilgrimage he spent
mostly at Lešno in Poland, where he wrote his
books on education and pansophy, i.e., a philosophical system of general knowledge. But
soon he travelled to Germany and Holland, from
there to England, from England to Sweden and
Poland again, returning to Lešno only after he
had been elected Bishop of the Unity. Then he
accepted the invitation of Prince Sigmund
Rákoczy and went to Hungary, where he
organised schools and produced for their use his
most popular book *Orbis Pictus*. Two years after
his return, Lešno was burnt down and for the
second time he lost his books and manuscripts,
especially those of a large *Czech and Latin
Dictionary* on which he had worked for more than
thirty years. He therefore again left Poland and
settled in Amsterdam where he received support
in his literary aims from Laurence de Geers, the
son of his old friend and protector in Sweden,
Louis de Geers. With his financial help he
published there the complete edition of his
educational works, a new edition of his
*Labyrinth*, some new books on ' pansophy ', some
polemic pamphlets and at last, feeling that his
life was approaching its end, two smaller books :
*The Sad Voice of a Frightened Herdsman* and
*Unum Necessarium*, in which he uttered a
farewell to his dispersed Church. He died at

Amsterdam in November, 1670, at the age of seventy-eight.

He was the last great author and spiritual leader of the Czech people in the dark period when it lost its independence. As he never abandoned the hope that it would recover this independence again, he prepared the way for its happier future, writing books in which he lay the foundations for a better education of those generations that were to come. In the meantime his native country was ravaged by nearly all the belligerent forces that had taken part in the Thirty Years' War. Its intellectual life was stopped, its schools were closed or latinised and Romanised, its literature almost died out. He saw all this material and spiritual catastrophe from afar, he felt it perhaps more intensely than many others among his compatriots, but he did not despair. When the Treaty of Westphalia was signed, and none of its articles mentioned the future of those thousands and thousands of the Czech Protestants and Brethren who lived like beggars in exile, he realised that there was no possibility for him and his contemporaries to see Bohemia and Moravia again. He also knew what they had to expect if they continued to live dispersed in foreign towns and villages. Nevertheless he wrote in the *Last Testament of that Dying Mother the Unity of the Bohemian Brethren* these memorable words : ' I also believe before

God that after the passing of the storms of wrath, brought down upon our heads by our sins, the rule over thine own possessions shall be restored to thee, O Czech people ! And for this hope do I make thee inheritor of everything, not only of all that I have inherited from my forefathers, and preserved notwithstanding the troublous and grievous times, but also of whatever increase I have received in any good work through the labour of my sons and the blessing of God '.

Two hundred and sixty eight years afterwards, Masaryk read his first message to the National Assembly of the new Republic. He began it with the same words to show how the present was closely connected with the past ; how the foundations laid by Komenský when the fortunes of his nation were at their lowest ebb were the same upon which the house of the new freedom was built.

# CHAPTER III

## DARKNESS AND DAWN

THE results of the defeat of the Bohemian Estates on the White Mountain in 1620 were more extensive and significant than those of any other defeat on record in Czech history. Not only did Bohemia lose her political independence, religious freedom and her previous prosperity, but what was worse for the further development of Czech civilisation and culture, the nation was deprived of its spiritual leaders and later even of those means which might have enabled it, after a shorter or longer period of suffering, to collect and utilise its resources. The Jesuits, who became the masters of the souls of the impoverished and enslaved peasants, suppressed all spiritual freedom and endeavoured to extirpate all memories of their happier past from the minds of the Czechs. They Romanised and latinised the schools, they persecuted all of whom they suspected of heresy, they searched for and burnt Czech books which seemed to them to be not quite orthodox, and as many of them were ignorant of the Czech language, they burnt rather more of them than was strictly necessary. One of them, called

Koniáš—a name which assumed nearly the same character among the Czechs as that of Herostratos among the Greeks—was accused of destroying about sixty thousand Czech books, and if we consider that there were many hundreds like him who worked with more or less success in the same way, we can easily imagine the effects of their labours.

But not only did they destroy older books, they also tried to produce new ones. It is difficult to say which side of their work was more ruinous to Czech literature. Koniáš himself wrote and published in the first half of the eighteenth century a book entitled *A Key to a More Complete Revelation of Heretical Errors*, which was called in a later edition *Index Librorum Prohibitorum Corrigendorum* (A List of Prohibited Books Which Have to be Improved). Such books as this were typical among the productions of the Jesuits and very often did not even rise to its level. The so-called Infernal Psalteries, i.e., books describing in vivid colours the everlasting tortures of the infidels after their death, could not elevate or substantially improve those who read them. And as the average of the popular literature was not much better, and the prayers, sermons or homilies did not always suffice to quench the spiritual thirst of their readers, it is natural that the situation of a Czech man or woman who had no access to any other literature

than that which the Jesuits produced or permitted to be produced, was most unenviable.

It is true that there were a few Roman Catholic
authors who had higher literary aims and wrote
books of a different kind, as for example,
chronicles, grammars, and treatises on ortho-
graphy; or, who, being themselves sterile,
translated or imitated German and Latin verse.
But because they possessed no ideas and little
erudition, and as their instrument, the Czech
language, was very imperfect, having been
thoroughly neglected for a long time, none of
their products possess scientific or artistic value.
Even those who regarded themselves as competent
judges, and compiled Czech grammars for their
less competent countrymen showed sometimes
such an elementary ignorance of their mother
tongue that they practically did more harm than
good. As the secondary and higher schools were
latinised, and in the second half of the eighteenth
century Germanised, the better educated people
learned to use Latin or German, and if they
wished to write books or pamphlets for those
Czechs who were educated in a similar way,
they wrote them in Latin and later on in German.
However, even they had to be careful not to
express their national feelings. For the Church
and the State controlled, through their censors,
all that was printed, and did not allow anything
to be published which might remind the Czechs

of their past independence and their great historical traditions; and if they allowed it, the truth had to be veiled or corrected in favour of the Roman Catholics and the ruling dynasty.

How far they went in this zeal is shown by the fact that the rigorous censors ordered the destruction even of the Bohemian Chronicle, by Æneas Sylvius, i.e., by Pope Pius II, simply because he writes in it about the Hussites, though from the Roman point of view and therefore mostly unfavourably. BOHUSLAV BALBÍN, a Jesuit, who, in the second half of the seventeenth century, produced a large Latin work called *Miscellanea Historica Regni Bohemiæ* (Historical Miscellanies of the Kingdom of Bohemia), had a similar experience when he wished to publish his smaller book, *Epitome Rerum Bohemicarum* (A Summary of Czech History). His assertion, which was founded on historical sources and was quite true, that the crown of Bohemia had not been hereditary but elective, and that the Czech language had, in previous centuries, been the only official language in Bohemia, was found so dangerous by the superior of his Order that he was banished to a provincial town and for several years was not permitted to continue printing his book. This punishment, however, did not cause him to change his mind. He preserved his sympathy with his country and his fellow-countrymen also in later years, as we see from his larger work which remained unfinished and unpublished during his life, and especially from his treatise *Dissertatio Apologetica pro Lingua Slavonica, Precipue Bohemica*, in which he defended the ancient Czech language from its slanderers, a language that he himself did not use, and perhaps even could not use, as a literary expression of his ideas and feelings.

This Apology, concluding with a fervent prayer to St. Venceslas that he might protect the Czech people and not allow it to perish, was written, like Balbín's other works, as an ' epitaph of Old Bohemia '. But Bohemia was not quite dead, and her grave-diggers did not permit the Apology to be published during the seventeenth century. Even as late as 1775, nearly a hundred years after the death of its author, it was confiscated by the Austrian authorities when it was printed for the first time.

The shackles which had restrained the national life of the Czechs for one hundred and fifty years now began to show signs of being loosened. The Western European ideas that in France had prepared the way for the Great Revolution, particularly the theism and rationalism of Locke and his followers, or of Voltaire and the Encyclopedists, penetrated slowly also into the benighted countries under the Austrian sceptre, and first influenced the more enlightened men among the scholars and friends of learning. Common interests united them into smaller and larger groups which assembled from time to time in hospitable houses, discussed new books and new thoughts and finally found methods of communicating their views to the public. In this way the first Bohemian periodicals of a scientific character were established. All of them were written for many years in German, because the contributors were not able to write in Czech, even though they were born Czechs, and the readers were accustomed to read in any other language except that of their own country. So deep was the fall of Bohemia about the middle of the eighteenth century.

Not long after the first of these periodicals had been started, the oldest Bohemian scientific society was also founded (about 1773). At the beginning it was called *The Private Learned Society* and assembled in the house of Ignatius Born, a nobleman who was specially interested in natural sciences. In its later development, however, the Society not only became public and changed its name into *Societas Scientiarum Bohemica*, but increasing the number of its members and the significance of its scientific publications, comprised before the end of the eighteenth century representatives of nearly all sciences. For some time its official languages were Latin and German, and in them its official publications were issued.

But in the course of the nineteenth century, when the Czech language had already acquired some freedom again and was no longer neglected by those who belonged to the educated classes, *Societas Scientiarum Bohemica* became a really Czech society, with Czech as its official language and mostly Czech publications. In this form it exists at the present day.

The University of Prague, which was nearly dead under the control of the Jesuits, began to stir when in the last quarter of the eighteenth century the Emperor Joseph II, under the influence of Western European ideas, enhanced intellectual freedom by abolishing the Jesuit Order in Austria. New men appeared among the professors, a new spirit awakened in the old colleges and directly and indirectly helped to rouse the nation from its apathy.

The reign of this ruler affected the national revival of the Czech people in a double way. He, like his contemporaries, Catherine II in Russia and Frederic II in Prussia, was an enlightened despot and like them a spiritual pupil of the French philosophers. Being imbued with their notions and theories, he got rid of the usual Roman Catholic clericalism of the Austrian monarchs. In accordance with his views he abolished such Orders and monasteries as he considered detrimental or at least useless to human society ; in the year 1781 he issued the so-called

Decree of Tolerance by which the Lutherans and Calvinists were given religious freedom. In some other respects he limited the power of the Roman Catholic Church, although, at the same time, he persecuted by rigorous regulations all the religious sects which were not expressly allowed by law. He granted the printers and publishers more liberty so that they could reprint older books or publish new books, periodicals or newspapers without being exposed to persecution; and finally he nearly abolished the serfdom of the peasants, making them feel that they also were men and not mere chattels of the selfish nobility.

All these reforms were accepted by the Czech people favourably, in particular by the lower classes and by those who had not yet accommodated their religious feelings to the prescribed doctrines of the Roman Catholic Church. The peasants preserved the memory of the Emperor Joseph as a prominent figure in their popular tales long after he had been dead. As the Czech racial elements were best conserved among the lower classes, and notably the peasants formed the best part of the Czech nation, all that raised them spiritually and helped them materially, raised and helped also the Czech nation.

But in a curious way even some of those regulations of Joseph II, which tended to bury the Czech language for ever, indirectly contributed to its revival. He was a stubborn centralist, following in this respect his mother, Maria Theresa. His ideal was to concentrate all the political power in Vienna and make his state so homogeneous that all its different nations should disappear and a new, the Austrian nation, be created, a nation speaking only German. He tried to realise this ideal by a new system of education which introduced the German language not only into universities and secondary schools but also into many elementary schools— not as a subject of teaching but as the language in which the instruction was to be given. And to show that it was meant quite seriously and that everybody had to learn German, he ordered that German should be the only language used even in the lowest law-courts, so that a great majority of people in non-German countries were practically excluded from justice. He did not live long enough to see that life was stronger than doctrine and that his imperial wishes could not effect what was contrary to nature. The people in Bohemia and Moravia felt consciously and unconsciously that the axe was laid at the roots of their national being and resisted the law, facilitating in this way the task of those brave defenders of their nationality who stood at the head of the defenceless masses.

They were not very numerous, and the results of their endeavours were rather insignificant at the beginning. They published German and

5

Czech apologies of their oppressed mother-tongue, showing their enemies as well as to their own countrymen that it did not deserve all the degradation and contempt which it shared with the other lost causes of the subjugated races ; they reprinted older books which might have been useful and interesting to Czech readers ; they compiled new pamphlets on such subjects as attracted the general attention at that time ; they founded the first Czech newspaper after a long period of absolute silence ; finally they wrote and played simple dramas and comedies which had more patriotic fervour than artistic or literary merits. Nowadays no one pays any attention to these unadorned products, except a few scholars who read them for special purposes ; but we must not underrate them from the historical point of view though we are quite conscious of their scanty æsthetic value.

More important than these early harbingers of the Czech national revival at the end of the eighteenth century were the men who laid the foundations of modern Czech science in the broadest sense of this word and who by their works contributed to a better knowledge partly of Czech history, partly of the Czech language. The rationalism of their own time could not produce true and original poetry; but it certainly produced sound scientific works. It did not yet possess what we may briefly call the historic sense, i.e., it did not understand the past in its own character; but it certainly possessed the critical faculty for which a historian or a philologist draws a distinction between realities and inventions, between facts and conjectures. And this was of great consequence to the further development of Czech literature and Czech culture; for both the Czech past and the Czech language were disfigured and contaminated by many slanders and inventions of that dark period which endeavoured to alter the soul of the Czech people and to destroy its language. Gelasius Dobner and Josef Dobrovský were those whose critical methods restored Czech history and purified the Czech language from all inorganic elements.

It is characteristic of the spirit of their time that both of them were ordained in the Roman Catholic Church and that both of them wrote their works in Latin and German. But so greatly did the last quarter differ from the earlier parts of the eighteenth century that neither of these circumstances prevented them from being tolerant freethinkers and true sons of their own nation.

GELASIUS DOBNER (1719-1790), who, in his private life was a headmaster of the College of the Piarist monks at Prague, is called ' the father of Czech history ', not so much on account of his *Monumenta historica Bohemiæ nusquam antehac edita* as because of his numerous treatises on older

Czech history, and especially of his critical notes to a Latin translation of an older Czech chronicle written in the sixteenth century by the Roman Catholic priest Václav Hájek of Libočany(*Wenceslai Hagek a Liboczan Annales Bohemorum,* 1762-1786). In this large work he analysed the tales of the annalist so thoroughly that Hájek ceased to be considered, as he really was, the chief authority on medieval Czech history. Hájek's admirers defended their idol but the voice of truth was too powerful and the younger generation of Czech historians preferred to follow Dobner.

His younger contemporary JOSEF DOBROVSKÝ (1753-1829) is one of the greatest scholars which the Czech nation ever produced. Born in Hungary, where his father served as a soldier, he was educated in Bohemia, at first among the Germans, then in the Czech part of the country. He spent one year as a novice in the Jesuit Order at Brno, but when the Order was abolished (1773), he went to the University of Prague to study theology. Very early, however, his attention was attracted more by philological and historical questions than by the dogmas and problems of the Roman Catholic Church. He studied Oriental, especially Semitic languages, but under the influence of his older friend, Václav Fortunát Durych, he turned his attention also to Old Slavonic and afterwards to other Slavonic languages and literatures. For several years he lived as a private tutor in noble families ; afterwards he was ordained and became a rector of one of those General Seminaries where Joseph II had the future priests educated according to his ideas ; and when, after the death of this Emperor, these institutes were dissolved, he returned with a small pension to Prague. There he spent the rest of his life as a private scholar, accepting from time to time the invitations of various nobles to live on their estates in the country.

This change was very fortunate for his scientific work. It provided him with plenty of leisure and enabled him to use large libraries as well as to come into contact with enlightened men at home and abroad. To ascertain what Czech or other Slavonic manuscripts and books were preserved in Sweden and in Russia he undertook, in the first years of this period of his life, a journey through Germany to Scandinavia and from there to Petrograd and Moscow ; but more important than the results of this were his great philological and historical works, besides many minor treatises on Slavonic languages and literatures which he produced during the next thirty years. He died at the age of seventy-six during a visit to Brno at the beginning of the year 1829.

John Bowring, who at that time translated poems from various European and in particular Slavonic languages into English and exchanged letters with many Slavonic scholars and poets, including Dobrovský, wrote in one of his articles that his critical and philosophical merits were perhaps not on a level with his knowledge. He did him a great injustice. Dobrovský was one of the best critical minds not only in Bohemia but also in Europe at the beginning of the nineteenth century. Without his acute critical faculties he could not have written his *Detailed Grammar of the Czech Language* (1809) in which he laid the foundations of the scientific research of the Czech language and showed the younger generation of Czech writers how to use their mother tongue in a proper manner ; he could not have written his *Institutiones Linguæ Slavicæ Dialecti Veteris* (1822), i.e., the first scientific Grammar of Old or Church Slavonic, a work which is considered as the foundation stone of Slavonic philology in the widest sense of this word; he could not have written a long series of articles on older Czech literature and history, which prepared the way for his later work, the *History of Older Czech literature* (1818), and for further investigations by his followers.

He was, however, much more than a great critic in the department of Czech and Slavonic philology. His versatility and personal charm raised him high above the average of contemporary scholars. Standing apart from all schools, he was the greatest teacher of the younger generation. Although he himself wrote mostly in German and

Latin, he taught them to write in Czech better than their fathers did ; using his cool critical mind in his studies, he enabled them not only to understand their Slavonic kinsmen and their own part more thoroughly but to love them more warmly ; and being himself attracted by a considerable variety of subjects, he gave them a great example of how one could be a perfect master even in writing short essays and studies.

He lived long enough to see the difference between his own generation and the younger one which was to take possession of his inheritance ; between the critical rationalism of the eighteenth and the Romantic Movement of the first half of the nineteenth centuries. This new literary, artistic, and partly scientific spirit migrated from one European country to another. Roughly speaking, we may say that it was born about the middle of the eighteenth century in England, where it grew very slowly, until it began to blossom half a century later. In Bohemia it appeared at the time of the Napoleonic wars, but its full development came two or three decades later. It was very favourable to the national aspirations of the Czechs, in the first place because it laid a strong emphasis on the importance of the emotions, and secondly, because it did not assume, like the rationalists of the previous period, that the poetic products of the lower classes or the common people were necessarily always worse than those of the educated writers. Dobrovský's rationalism led him to believe that it was hardly possible to create a new Czech literature of a higher standard, and that it was almost impossible to write scientific books in the Czech language. But the enthusiasm of the Romantic School not only disposed of all such doubts, but being guided by feeling, it tried to create a new Czech poetry as well as a new Czech science. The romantic writers did not despise the simple folk-songs ; on the contrary, they liked them, imitated them and thus stimulated the increasing revival of the national spirit. Once or twice they were misled by their fervour, but on the whole their success converted Dobrovský also, and in the last years of his life he began to write philological treatises in Czech.

JOSEF JUNGMANN (1773-1847) was the most prominent figure in the Romantic School during the first period of its development. He was the son of a peasant from Central Bohemia, and he had to struggle with the German language which was then the only medium for acquiring a good education. It was quite unknown to him before he went to a town-school, and by the time he had mastered it, he was almost Germanised like many others of his companions. He stammered, as he tells us, when, as a young man, he was invited to some rustic festivities, and tried to deliver a speech in his mother tongue. One of the country-girls, his relative, mocked his bad pronunciation of common words and his incorrect construction of simple sentences, and her timely derision prevented a gifted mind from being lost to the Czech nation. From then onwards he took great pains with the study of his mother language and at last became one of its most competent masters. He studied law but afterwards preferred to become a teacher at a secondary school in a country town and later on at Prague, where he was appointed headmaster of the oldest Gymnasium (Public School). He died in the year 1847, honoured and esteemed by his nation.

In his youth he wrote verses, but with indifferent success. More important than his own poems are his later translations from various languages, by which he wished firstly to show that the Czech language, although persecuted and neglected for nearly two centuries, was able to express the highest ideas and the most poetic images as well as other languages, and secondly, to create models of poetic diction for the use of younger Czech writers. The most notable among his achievements of this kind is his translation of Milton's *Paradise Lost*, published in the year 1811. He was not a great poet like Milton, and though he could convey adequately the thoughts and feelings, he could not reproduce the supreme poetic art of the original; nevertheless, what he did was a remarkable achievement, especially if we consider the backward condition in which he found the Czech language.

To make it as perfect as possible was the chief aim of his literary life. He wrote articles in which he admonished and animated his countrymen to take more care of this inheritance of their ancestors. When in 1816 the Austrian Government allowed Czech to be introduced in some Bohemian schools, not as the language of instruction but only as a voluntary subject, he published the so-called *Slovesnost*, a book, the object of which was to teach Czech pupils the main rules of Poetics and the typical productions of Czech and other Slavonic literatures. Some years later he produced a large *History of Czech literature*, a work which resembled more a bibliography than a real history, but for this reason was very valuable at that time, as it showed the general reader the quantity of Czech literary productions in the past and served as a source of information to scholars during the whole of the nineteenth century. But among all his works the *Dictionary of the Czech and German languages* in five big folio volumes (1834-1839) is the most important and valuable. There were several Czech-German Dictionaries before his, but none of the same size and none based on such wide and thorough knowledge. Jungmann had to study the older literature that was preserved largely in manuscripts; he had to study the language of the common people. In many cases he introduced new expressions which he borrowed mostly from other Slavonic languages, and thus he contributed to the development of the so-called Slavonic solidarity in Czechoslovakia. He also tried to investigate the historical development of single words and their meanings as far as possible and so to produce a work which would show how the Czech language had changed from the oldest times to the first half of the nineteenth century. At the present day, after new sources of knowledge have been opened and new methods of investigation created, the Dictionary of Jungmann is antiquated in some respects; but as a whole it will always remain a monument of Czech scholarship and will be always remembered as one of the main sources from which many of his younger contemporaries derived their knowledge of their mother tongue.

Although he was more a scholar than a poet, his literary character grew up under the influence of the Romantic Movement and therefore sometimes opposed the rigorous critical nature of Dobrovský who represents the older generation of the purer rationalists. The difference between them was emphasised most strikingly when the so-called *Manuscripts of Králové Dvůr* and *Zelená Hora* were discovered. In the year 1817 Václav Hanka, a pupil of Dobrovský in Slavonic philology, but a pupil of Jungmann in the romantic spirit, found, or at least declared that he had found, a parchment manuscript in the tower of the church at Králové Dvůr, a town in north-eastern Bohemia. His discovery created a great sensation, as the twelve parchment leaves contained eight epic and six lyric poems which, to judge by the character of the letters and of the language, dated as far back as the thirteenth century. And this was very acceptable to the romantics who were deeply interested in medieval poetry, especially as the poems of the Manuscript of Králové Dvůr supported their own views of Old Czech poetry and culture in general, and secondly, because the Manuscript itself apparently was only a small remnant of a large collection of Czech poems which, to the irreparable damage of Czech literature, had been lost. Hanka did not announce his discovery immediately to the Czech public, but only to some of his friends, and he awaited Dobrovský's opinion. When Dobrovský, deceived by its very skilful imitation of the medieval writing, gave his verdict that the Manuscript was genuine, Hanka's friend and probable collaborator, Linda, wrote the first public notice about the important discovery. Then, encouraged by their success, they produced another manuscript which was afterwards called the Manuscript of Zelená Hora, because Hanka alleged that it had been found in the castle of this name in southern Bohemia. It contained two fragments of epic poems, one being an Old Czech decree of domestic law, while the other described Libuša's judgment on two litigant brothers. Those responsible for the Manuscript wished to create the impression that it had been written in the ninth century. This time, however, Dobrovský was more cautious, and immediately deciding that it was a forgery, he made no secret of his opinion. But as other Czech writers and patriots were of a different opinion and welcomed the pretended discovery more or less enthusiastically, Hanka and his collaborators recovered their courage, and thus during the following decade several other forgeries, more of a philological than a poetical character, made their appearance. Not all of them were accepted with the same fervour as the Manuscript of Králové Dvůr; but on the whole there were more believers than sceptics among the Czech scholars, and therefore the question whether the so-called Old Czech Manuscripts were genuine or not remained unsettled for more than half a century, until the first generation of professors in the renovated Czech University of Prague came to another conclusion than the majority of their fathers and grandfathers. A new research persuaded them that not only the lesser Manuscripts but also those of Králové Dvůr and Zelená Hora were falsifications by Hanka, his friend Linda and partly perhaps by Václav Alois Svoboda.

Investigaticns by the experts proved that the
authors of the falsified poems had drawn a great
deal of their vocabulary from various sources of
earlier and later Czech literature and that their
productions contained many words in such forms
and with such meanings as could not be found in
other Czech works of undisputedly ancient origin.
As a result of the demonstrations of these critics,
at the head of whom were Professor Gebauer and
Professor Masaryk, no serious scholar now defends
the authenticity of the Manuscripts.

The Manuscripts of Králové Dvůr and
Zelená Hora aroused great interest abroad also
and they were translated, at least in selections,
into many European languages. This is not
surprising if we consider that they appeared in a
time which, more than any other, was interested
in medieval folk-songs and was easily deceived
by James Macpherson, William Henry Ireland,
and other literary forgers of the second half of the
eighteenth and the beginning of the nineteenth
centuries. When it was discovered that the
Manuscripts were spurious their glory diminished
very rapidly, perhaps more rapidly than they
really deserved; for though they were not of
ancient but of modern origin, Josef Linda, who
probably composed the longer epic poems of the
MS of Králové Dvůr—Hanka dressed them in
their old Czech garment—was talented enough
to produce in them the best Czech epic poetry

during the second decade of the nineteenth
century. Some of their mythical figures im-
pressed themselves strongly upon the mind of the
younger generation, as we see from the works
of such distinguished Czech exponents of the arts
as the composer Smetana, the sculptor Myslbek
and the painters Mánes and Aleš.

Their influence on Czech literature was more
limited. It would be difficult to name an original
poet who was greatly influenced by the lyric songs
on the ' garland ', or the ' cuckoo ', or the ' rose ',
or the 'skylark ', or by the epics on Záboj, Zbyhoň,
Jaroslav, Čestmír, or Beneš Heřmanóv. Only
in the works of some minor poets do we find traces
of them, but more in their poetic diction than in
their inner character. Poets who possessed more
originality went their own way ; and if there is
any similarity between them and the manuscripts, we may explain it more by the common
taste of their time than by a direct imitation ; for
both the authors of the Manuscripts and the
poets were children of the same Romantic period
which not only nourished them with the same
ideas but endowed them with similar qualities.

The beginnings of Czech poetry at the period
of the national revival were rather precarious,
and it took three or four decades before a new
poetic diction was created. All the endeavours
of the first poetic school at that time aimed at
this inevitable problem, and if we still remember

Antonín Jaroslav Puchmajer and his friends or collaborators, it is because of their merits in this respect rather than for their artistic achievements. For the same reason we sometimes speak of M. Z. Polák's *Sublimity of Nature* (1819) as an important poem of Jungmann's literary school although our critical instinct tells us that it was more an artistic experiment than real poetry.

The first man in the nineteenth century whom we may call a poet is JAN KOLLÁR (1793-1852). His cradle stood in a Slovak village at the foot of the Carpathian Mountains. He received his education in various parts of Slovakia before he went, at the age of twenty-four, to Jena in Germany in order to complete his theological studies there. Both the year and the place became very important in his spiritual development. It was in 1817, two years after Waterloo and only a few weeks before the German Protestants, and especially the students of Jena, celebrated the tercentenary of Martin Luther. Their religious and political enthusiasm, their joy at the new freedom, their romantic dreams of the future union of all Germans in one large State, and especially the philosophical views of some professors whose lectures he attended, influenced his susceptible mind very strongly, giving him one of the chief impulses to his later idea of Slavonic solidarity. Several months after his arrival he became acquainted with the daughter of a pastor in a neighbouring village. He fell passionately in love with her and would have married her if her mother, after the death of her husband, had allowed her to accompany the young clergyman to a country which she considered to be quite uncivilised. As Kollár could not remain in Germany because he wished to work at home for his own people, he had to take leave of his beloved and return to Slovakia alone. This separation, and later some incorrect news that his Mína was dead, caused him to portray the pastor's daughter as an immortal being, the daughter of the goddess Sláva who was for him a personification of the whole Slavonic race. And as such he incorporated her in his large poem *Daughter of Sláva*, the original parts of which consisted of love sonnets written during his stay in Jena. Many years afterwards when he lived as a pastor of the Slovak Protestant Community in Budapest, he heard that Mína was alive. He offered her his hand for the second time, was accepted and brought her as his wife to Hungary. His life was not particularly prosperous or quiet. The persecution by the Hungarian Government on account of his Slavonic patriotism and of his books, in which he advocated Slavonic solidarity, rendered his stay in Budapest more and more difficult until, during the Hungarian revolution of 1848, he was obliged to leave his house secretly in order to avoid being murdered by the rebels. A year afterwards, when the revolution was suppressed, he was appointed to the chair of Slavonic archæology at the University of Vienna. But he died there a little more than two years later before he had finished his archæological works which were to emphasise his fantastic views of the centres and civilisation of the Slavonic peoples in the Middle Ages.

These books, of which only one was published, did not add much to his literary fame. On the contrary, they would have damaged it very seriously if the critical world had expected a scientific research from a poet. His younger contemporary, Karel Havlíček, very aptly remarked that Kollár was a philologist or archæologist in his poems, and a poet in his philology and archæology. He alluded especially to the last two songs of his *Daughter of Sláva* and to the *Explanations*, which the poet considered necessary for making his verses more comprehensible to the general reader. But though the value and influence of his archæological hypotheses and fictions was very small, the influence of his long poem as regards the idea of Slavonic solidarity and the revival of the Slavonic nations was of quite fundamental importance. It became, and for many years remained, a real Bible of all the subjugated Slavonic nations.

It grew rather slowly. In its original form

it was a small collection of sonnets and other poems, published two years after the poet's return from Germany and containing mostly love sonnets on Mína. Three years afterwards (1824) he produced—for the first time under the title of the *Daughter of Sláva*—an enlarged edition, divided into three cantos, which he designated with the names of the rivers Saale, Elbe and Danube respectively. The erotic element prevails in them; but in many places it recedes into the background, particularly in those sonnets where the daughter of a German pastor becomes the daughter of Sláva and where the poet, travelling like a new Childe Harold through the countries which are, or at least were, inhabited by the Slavs, laments the losses they have suffered from Germanisation and Magyarisation during the preceding centuries. Occasionally he expresses his views of human life, in other places again he becomes a prophet, admonishing his countrymen with fiery words to live in concord and to cherish patriotism. The whole is preceded by an elegy in elegiac couplets, the most powerful lyric written by Kollár. 'Here', he exclaims pathetically in the opening lines where he describes himself as standing on the banks of the Elbe in a country which was formerly inhabited by Slavs, ' here before my eyes dissolved in tears that country lies which once was the cradle, now is the tomb of my nation. . . .

Oh, ye bygone ages, surrounding me as with night ! Oh, country that art an image of glory and shame ! From the treacherous Elbe to the plains of the faithless Vistula, from the Danube to the devouring waves of the Baltic—there resounded once the harmonious language of the brave Slavs, but it is mute now, having been silenced by hatred . . .'. And then he charges the Germans with this offence which cries to heaven for vengeance, declaring that he who forges shackles to enslave others is himself a slave, whether he restrains their language or their limbs. But in spite of all the hardships and losses of the Slavonic tribes in Germany he will not bemoan the fate of his race, he does not despair. For ' not from a mournful eye, but from a diligent hand new hope will blossom ; thus only even evil may turn to good. A crooked way may mislead men only, not the whole of mankind. . . . Time changes everything ; the intentions of centuries may be overthrown in a day '.

It was this powerful elegy with its finale, breathing hope and energy, which affected the minds of Kollár's contemporaries most deeply ; it affects the Czech mind even to-day, after time has really changed many things. It is much finer than the last two cantos of the poem which Kollár added to the enlarged first three in its complete edition. In order to be consistent he chose as their titles the names of the rivers Lethe and Acheron. He remembered Dante's *Divine Comedy* and wished to create a Slavonic *Paradise* and *Inferno* where he might place those men and women whose good deeds had helped the Slavs, or whose crimes had brought misfortune upon them. His imagination, however, was not strong enough, and the result of his endeavours was not only far below Dante's, but also below his own level in the first half of the *Daughter of Sláva*. The didactic note of his additional verses could not replace the loss of the vigorous pathos which concerned the readers of the opening elegy.

But on the whole, his poem, both in its successful and unsuccessful sonnets, embodied the doctrine of the solidarity of the Slavonic nations so completely that his later explanations in a treatise and in sermons, dealing with the same subject, were almost unnecessary to the public, though they greatly contributed to the development of this idea among the intellectuals. Kollár's pathetic sorrow at the humiliation of the Slavs in his own time, when only the Russians had an independent state, and his firm conviction of their future revival and prosperity gave an immense impulse to racial consciousness, not only among his own countrymen but also among their kinsmen far beyond the boundaries of Bohemia or Slovakia. His famous sonnet, beginning with the words : ' What will become of us Slavs a century hence ? What of all Europe ? ' sounded like an utterance of a prophet who awakened his sleeping brothers and sisters to a new life—not only in the narrow sense of nationalism, but at the same time in the much broader and deeper sense of humanity. He was the man who said, in one of his epigrams : ' Whenever you say *Slav*, always think of *man* '; who taught that nationalism without humanity was pernicious and that even a great nation would be cursed by mankind if it forgot that *man* was the end, but German or Frenchman only a stepping stone to the final goal. His voice was heard by those who came after him, and his opinion was shared by the best representatives and spiritual leaders of his nation, such as Palacký, Havlíček and Masaryk.

# CHAPTER IV

## FROM THE NATIONAL REVIVAL TO THE NEW POLITICAL INDEPENDENCE

### I

THE idea of Slavonic solidarity, itself a product of the Romantic movement, influenced Czech literature of the Romantic period in several respects. It had been current since the days of Dobrovský's travels, waiting until someone would express it in a more accessible form. This was done by Kollár in his celebrated poem. But the interest in the Slavonic nations was soon exhibited in other aspects also. Some able men among the Czech patriots began to study the simple songs and legends of the lower classes of their own as well as of other Slavonic peoples, seeing in them, and not without justification, more original elements of their culture than in the literary achievements of the middle classes. Others again explored the past history of the Slavs in order to make their countrymen and kinsmen better acquainted with the deeds of their ancestors and to trace in ancient times the originality which their contemporaries were searching for among the peasants and shepherds of their day.

These two aspects of interest are represented in Czech literature of the first half of the nineteenth century especially by four prominent names. The poets Čelakovský and Erben cultivated folk-lore, the scholars Šafařík and Palacký historical research. A little aside from them stood the woman novelist Božena Němcová and the publicist Karel Havlíček, whose outlook was directed more towards the future than the past; but both of them were prompted by strong sympathies with the common people. It is characteristic of their generation that its poets are also scholars and that scholars try to be poets, too. Versatility is the motto of their time; it is the necessity of their nation, the unfavourable conditions of whose existence often compelled Czech patriots to take upon their shoulders more, and sometimes heavier burdens than would otherwise be desirable.

FRANTIŠEK LADISLAV ČELAKOVSKÝ (1799-1852), like most of the Czech writers in the nineteenth century, was a child of the countryside. Born in a small town of western Bohemia he went to Prague to study in the faculty of arts after he had finished his secondary education, and after he had abandoned the original plan of his parents, who had wanted him to become a priest. Having left the university, he was a private tutor for some time, then an editor, afterwards a librarian, and at last a professor of Slavonic philology in

Breslau, from where he returned to Prague, only three years defore his death. Early in his youth he studied German poets and critics, in particular Goethe, Herder and Lessing; then he turned his attention to the Slavonic languages and literatures, but especially to the folk-songs of the Slavonic nations. At first he collected and translated them into Czech. Later on, when he had become familiar with their characteristic features, he imitated them in his own poems, or rather created original poetry in the spirit of folk-songs. His two books: the *Echo of Russian Songs* and the *Echo of Czech Songs* are his greatest poetic achievements. Their originality is in the consummate manner in which he reproduced the national spirit of Russia or Bohemia in short epics and lyrics, composed in the manner of the native poetic products of the Russians and Czechs. Brave deeds of mythical heroes are depicted in them as suggestively as the glorious events of contemporary Russian history; the ardent desire of a soldier for his love or the modest happiness of his home as skilfully as the sorrow of a bereaved maiden; joy as well as grief, mockery as well as indignation and anger, losses as well as hopes, little realities as well as consoling dreams. All is clad in a lucid form, seasoned with the characteristics of Russian or Czech popular styles and with the masterly strokes of a born artist.

More subjective is his later work, *The Hundred-leaved Rose*, a collection of one hundred short lyrics. In its first part he expresses his love for the lady who later became his wife; in the second he tries to develop his philosophical views on life and nature. But the artistic output of this philosophising is rather scanty.

Much more vigorous and effective are his *epigrams*. His cleverness, his wit, his critical capacity, and the training he had received in the school of Martial and Lessing made him able to produce about three hundred of these short pieces, and many of them quite excellent. He liked to dress the wisdom of life in concise and terse language. He therefore also liked proverbs, and his *Collection of Slavonic proverbs*, which was published in the year of his death, is one of the earliest and most graceful monuments of the popular wisdom of the Slavs.

His younger contemporary, KAREL JAROMÍR ERBEN (1811-1870), resembled him as a man and writer in several ways. Like Čelakovský he changed his occupations in life until he became keeper of the records of the city of Prague; like him he passed from poetry to scientific research; like him, he was greatly interested in folk-songs and folk-tales of the Czechs and other Slavs. He began his literary career by collecting them. His *Czech Folk-songs and Popular Sayings* and his *Slavonic Folk-tales* belong to the first and best of their kind in Czech literature, so as his later editions of the works of Štítný, Hus, Bartoš Písař, Harant and other productions of older Czech prose and poetry were models of accurate scholarship for a long time.

The collecting of popular poetry influenced his own poetic power very strongly. Before he felt the charm of the popular tales, songs and ballads, he composed short poems of indifferent value, and a comedy which differed very little from the average comedies of that time. But after his soul had been stirred by the artistic spirit of the people, he created a work which will always be one of the ornaments of Czech literature. The chief merit of his *Garland of National Folktales* is comprised in twelve ballads the matter-subject of which, or at least some of their motives, he found in the rich traditional literature of the Slavonic peoples. He possessed the gift of transforming the elements discovered in anonymous productions of the peasants and shepherds into something higher not only from the artistic but also from the ethical point of view. We find in them the same beings as in the folk-tales : water spirits and witches, ghosts and devils, midnight apparitions and skeletons. We find in them the same actions, proceeding from the same causes : murders, suicides, treason, blasphemies, various sorts of faithlessness or greediness. We find in them the same simplicity of expression, the same terseness of language. If we critically analyse his poems we discover how judiciously he sifted his elements, how he combined them in order to increase their effectiveness, how he deepened the moral feelings of his characters to make them more human. His seduced or blaspheming girls, his contrite criminals, his greedy mothers and despairing daughters are not only men and women with distinctive features but human types at the same time—types that cannot be crushed by natural or supernatural forces however strong, because their souls have power enough to overcome them morally by repentance and purification. Some of his ballads are little tragedies as to their structure and the resulting impression they leave in the mind of the reader—tragedies which, according to the rule of Aristotle, relieve and elevate ; epic dramas with interspersed lyric descriptions of landscapes which only the eye of the poet could catch and fix with so much simplicity and beauty.

The *Garland* was the only poetical work which Erben produced. When he published it (1853) he was already deeply immersed in historical and literary research, preparing his important editions of older works and documents. In this department of his activity he was the pupil of the great historian Palacký.

Since the days of Dobner and Dobrovský history had become a favourite subject of study among the Czechs. No other branch of knowledge and literature could better help the patriots than that which demonstrated to their countrymen the glorious past of their nation, or which endeavoured to trace the development of the Slavonic race as far back as possible. We can discern these two branches of historical research in Bohemia already in some essays and articles of Dobrovský. They reached the high water-mark in Šafařík and Palacký.

PAVEL JOSEF ŠAFAŘÍK (1795-1861) considered himself rather a philologist than a historian though his university education extended also over the sphere of history, and, indeed, his main work is historical. Like Kollár, he was born in Slovakia, like him, but some time earlier, he went to Jena in Germany to study Protestant theology; being, however, attracted by literature, classical philology, history and philosophy, he devoted himself to these subjects and became afterwards a master at a Serbian Gymnasium (secondary school) in Novi Sad (Neusatz) in southern Hungary. There he directed his attention to Serbian and other Slavonic literatures and wrote two works on them in German. But the climate did not agree with his health, and the separation from the world of scholarship hindered his literary efforts. After fourteen years spent at Novi Sad, he was glad to receive an offer made by his friends in Bohemia, and moved to Prague.

He had, however, to struggle with material difficulties, and when at last a better official situation delivered him from these troubles, his health was broken and did not allow him to carry out all his plans.

Even his greatest work that made his name known in the whole learned world and was translated into three foreign languages, his *Slavonic Antiquity* (1837), remained unfinished. He never wrote the second part, in which he had intended to deal with the cultural history of the Slavonic nations, chiefly because his other duties did not leave him time enough to undertake all the preliminary work that was necessary. But the two volumes of the first part in which he solved such problems as when the Slavs came to Europe, where they settled in the first centuries after their arrival, and how they politically developed down to the year 988, were a monument of scholarship in themselves. As a Russian critic said, they overthrew the contemporary views on many of these questions, surprising the experts by the rich sources on which he drew, and by his detailed criticism of them. For these reasons his *Slavonic Antiquity* remains a great work also to-day although many of his theses were disposed of or improved by later research which relied on new branches of knowledge that were not accessible to Šafařík. His book was highly praised by his contemporaries, to whom it presented for the first time a complete and skilfully drawn picture of their most ancient history.

There was only one other work at that time which produced a similar impression—the *History of the Czech People*, by Šafařík's friend Palacký.

When these two men were youths, the one twenty and the other twenty-three, they wrote and published together a small book in which they expressed their views on Czech prosody, defending the old Greek and Latin metrical rules against Dobrovský who recommended stress as the chief factor in good Czech verse. Both imagined that they were poets and accordingly made or translated poems. Both arrived afterwards at the conclusion that their poetical gifts were rather limited, and devoted their lives to history.

FRANTIŠEK PALACKÝ (1798-1876) was born in eastern Moravia, but being a Protestant (like Kollár and Šafařík) he was sent by his father, a village schoolmaster, to Slovakia where the Protestants enjoyed more freedom of conscience than in Moravia or Bohemia. There he was educated in a country grammar school and afterwards in the Protestant college at Bratislava, the present capital of Slovakia. For a time he thought of going to Asia and becoming a missionary among the heathen. But a profound study of philosophy and æsthetics, conversations with an intelligent and highly educated lady whose family he visited as a private tutor, and the memorable evenings he spent in the house of her cousin where a few young gifted scholars used to discuss interesting problems of philosophy, art and literature, induced him to alter his plans. He learned foreign languages, studied great works of several literatures, wrote valuable treatises on æsthetics, and finally, under the influence both of the past of his nation and of some eminent historical works which he read, he resolved to become an historian himself. He never went to a university, but by private reading and contact with scholars at Bratislava and later in Vienna he acquired such thorough and universal knowledge that no university could teach him anything more. Following the invitation of Dobrovský, he came at the age of twenty-five to Prague in order to study there the sources for his projected History of the Hussite movement, in which he saw one of the greatest epochs of his nation. His talent and unusual knowledge, his winning personality and the patronage of Dobrovský brought him in contact with some enlightened noblemen who supported him in his literary efforts. Several among them stood at the head of the National Czech Museum, an institution corresponding in some ways to the British Museum in London. Thus he became closely connected also with the Museum Committee and, with their consent and help, could establish a scientific Quarterly, called *Časopis Musea Království českého* (Journal of the Museum of the Kingdom of Bohemia) which he made the centre of all literary life in Bohemia and the chief depository of his first historical and critical essays. This periodical has been published ever since, being now the oldest Czech review of that kind. Later on another institution was founded at his recommendation by the Society of the National Czech Museum, the so-called Matice Česká, or an organisation which was to issue elaborate literary and scientific works that no private publisher was able or willing to undertake. If it had not been for this, the large *Dictionary* of Jungmann, or the *Slavonic Antiquity* of Šafařík would not have been printed at that time.

But these were only the first results of his organising ability which increased with the tasks he had to master, and ultimately made him, so to speak, the chief organiser of the whole nation. He not only became a leader in learned or other important national societies and committees, not only wrote the first great national History, but when the year 1848 altered the constitution of Austria for a short time, he became the political leader and spokesman of his nation, creating for it a new political programme. When he died, the whole Czech nation mourned his loss and sent its

7

representatives from all parts of the country to accompany him to his last resting-place.

Palacký is one of the most prominent figures in the whole course of Czechoslovak history. When he came to Prague, and in the society of his learned protectors and friends there heard sceptical remarks about the possibility of a Czech national revival, he opposed them and declared : ' I at least, even if I were born a gipsy and the last member of my people, should consider it my duty to make every endeavour to help it to leave an honourable name in the history of mankind '. He preserved this spirit during his whole life. He was a dualist, believing that human life was an everlasting struggle between soul and body, between spirit and matter ; that a desire to over-come this dualism lived in the human soul ; at the same time, however, there was a consciousness that no such thing was possible ; nevertheless that this desire revealed itself through some ideal which man formed for himself and which com-pelled him to follow it, and following it, to improve not only himself but also his fellow-men, his nation and, through the nation, mankind. He created a special term for this desire, calling it *božnost*, i.e., longing after God, a longing to come nearer to God. And he also believed that this longing was identical with the highest power not only of man but also of nations and of human race. Even a small nation can be pervaded by it and then achieve much that is great.

On this philosophy he based his greatest literary achievement, his *History of the Czech People in Bohemia and Moravia* (from the earliest times to the year 1526, i.e., to the election of the first king of the Habsburg dynasty). The greatness of this work is not only in the immense preparatory researches he had to undertake before he could write the first line of the first chapter; not only in its perfect literary form; not only in the profound scholarship he displays from beginning to end : its merit lies above all in his deep insight into the character of his nation, in the manner in which he traces and expounds its historical development, interpreting the present by the past in order to demonstrate to his countrymen, and to the world as well, that physical strength was not the chief cause which made the Czechs victorious during the Hussite wars, but the zealous idealism, the morality and higher culture of the middle and lower classes of the Czech people at that time. The conclusion at which he arrives is that the Czech nation, in spite of its numerical inferiority, was always strong whenever it served an ideal, and through that ideal the higher good of mankind, its progress and morality, and on the other hand that it always became weak whenever it lost its faith in its ideals. This inference induced him to believe that his people could recover its spiritual strength again if it were animated by a new ardour, a new idealism. In other words, according to him, to be a Czech in the best sense meant to do some higher duty than to live but one's private or national life without thinking of others ; it meant to be an altruist and not in any way an egoist. There lies the educational value of his History, of his essays and speeches, the richest legacy he left to his nation and perhaps to others as well.

He constructed his political programme also on a very broad basis of national culture, considering a good education of all classes the noblest and best weapon in the hands of an oppressed people. He therefore always placed his literary work above his political activity ; he therefore often reminded his countrymen how important it was to take care of those institutions which supported the moral and mental improvement of the nation ; therefore, too, in taking leave of his compatriots, he declared in his last public speech, only a month before his death ; ' Now it is necessary to educate ourselves and to work in accordance with our enlightened minds. Feeling that my death is very near, this is the only legacy which I leave to my nation '.

Fortunately he found followers who understood his programme and endeavoured to put it into practice. None of them was keener and abler than the young journalist KAREL HAVLÍČEK, who assumed the pseudonym of BOROVSKÝ (1821-1856). This man who was destined by his parents to become a priest, was expelled from the Seminary at Prague because, according to the authorities, his knowledge was found insufficient and his principles unsatisfactory. In reality his character was too strong, his spirit too free and desirous of knowledge to be contented with what a seminary for priests could give him. He resolved to become a writer and as his education was German, he studied Jungmann's large Dictionary in order to improve his diction. In Russia, where he spent a year and a half as a private tutor, he did not find what he expected. His mind was too critical not to perceive the immense deficiencies of absolutism, and thus, returning home, he brought with him, besides a great quantity of fresh knowledge and a deep love of Gogol's humour and realism, some dozens of sharp epigrams against the oppression by State and Church. He utilised his knowledge partly in sketching his realistic and pungent *Pictures from Russia*, partly in his translations from Gogol, partly in his later satirical poems, but foremost as a basis for his progressive political efforts. He, one of the greatest Russophiles born in Bohemia, saw as a youth of twenty-two the whole misery of the Russian people under the rule of Czarism, and he understood the ' Russian sorrow ' better than anyone else among his countrymen at that time.

His unusual literary and political talent was revealed shortly after his return in the critical articles which he contributed to the periodical *Česká Včela* and still more in the manner in which he transformed the mediocre newspaper, the *Pražské Noviny* (The Prague News), the editor of which he was appointed, into an organ that voiced the political conscience of his country. Two years afterwards, in 1848, being not quite twenty-seven years old, he became, next to Palacký, the most popular and important political leader of the Czech nation. He left the editorship of the *Pražské Noviny* and founded his own organ, *Národní Noviny* (The National News), the first independent political journal in the Czech language. For some time, until the new Austrian Constitution was suspended by the young Emperor Franz Joseph I and the diet of Kroměříž was dispersed by soldiers, he was also a deputy; but he preferred his pen to his speeches and gladly returned to his regular occupation as a journalist. His activity, however, was in great disfavour with the Austrian Government, not only because he criticised their misrule but also because he very ably instructed the Czech public in the elementary knowledge of politics. For this reason his journal was suppressed, and when, some months later, he established another paper, called *Slovan* (The Slav), number after number was confiscated, he himself was expelled from Prague to the country

and then brought by the Public Prosecutor for
trial as a political criminal at Kutná Hora. He
was unanimously acquitted as quite innocent of
the charge, but he was arrested shortly afterwards by order of the Austrian minister Bach
and sent to the Tyrol where he remained interned
for more than three years. His wife and daughter
followed him next year, but being unable to
endure the rough climate of the mountainous
country, they returned home. He lingered on
in exile and when he was ultimately allowed to
leave Brixen and go back to Bohemia, he found
his wife dead. His own health was so bad that in
July, 1856, not yet thirty-five years of age, he
followed his wife as a victim of political
persecution.

During his life he published only two books
of his own : *The Spirit of the Národní Noviny*,
i.e., a selection from his political articles written
for his journal, and *The Epistles from Kutná
Hora*, containing his most important essays on
some problems both of a religious and political
nature which he published for the first time in the
periodical *Slovan*. These books are classics of
their kind. For acute criticism of public affairs,
and lucid exposition of difficult problems they
have no equals in contemporary Czech literature.
The same high standard is reached also by the bulk
of his journalistic work which was collected and
published in several volumes long after his death.

Although the subjects are now mostly out of date, one can read his articles with pleasure and profit even to-day, not as political ' leaders ', but merely as good political literature.  Nobody else could have educated his readers to citizenship so ably as Havlíček.

He was not a man of imagination.  *Things* he observed, of *things* he wrote in his prose and verse.  He was the first great realist in Czech literature.  But this does not mean that he was satisfied with things perceived.  His penetrating intellect saw faults so fully and deeply that he was often roused to irony and found relief only in producing caustic epigrams or satires.  As to his *epigrams* he learnt much from Martial, Pushkin, Lessing and Logau whose ' Inscriptions ' he studied and partly translated during his sojourn in Russia and afterwards in his exile.  But he was very far from being a mere imitator.  He is indeed a master himself, one of the best of modern epigrammatists.  Epigrams were to him mostly ' small vessels into which he poured his rage ', as he said, ' to prevent its eating his heart away '.  He did not produce them for the sake of showing his wit ; they were generally the result of his personal experience, of his personal feeling or deep conviction, of his extraordinary critical capacity, and hence they have retained their freshness until to-day.  Like the epigrams of Pushkin in Russia they circulated only privately, being copied by his friends, because many of them could not be published in those reactionary times.

The same destiny befell also his *satires* in verse, the *Baptism of St. Vladimír*, the *Tyrol Elegies*, and the *King Lávra*. In the first he made an important event of old Russian history the pretext for his scornful criticism of the contemporary Russian and Austrian absolutism. In the *Tyrol Elegies* he depicted with irony and humour borne on an undercurrent of deep feeling, his arrest and deportation to the Tyrol, while his *King Lávra* changed the old tale of a king who was ashamed of his long ears into a popular ballad with flashes of humour and some sidelights on the highest representatives of contemporary society.

During his exile he could not write as he wished because he needed that equilibrium of mind which was to him one of the chief conditions of good literary work. His rich talent was not allowed to develop fully. But however fragmentary his life and work, his great personality ennobles them both. To the following generations he became a symbol, one of those heroes who live in the centre of their nation's idealism. Thus he has lived for more than sixty years and will live for ages to come.

Twenty years before his death occurred the death of another young writer who did not complete his life's work. This was the poet

KAREL HYNEK MÁCHA (1810-1836), who belonged to the generation of Kollár and Čelakovský ; but as a poet he was greatly in advance of his time. For this reason he could not be understood by his contemporaries, whose criticism either neglected him, or was unjust to him. Not until' twenty years after his death did he begin to be acknowledged as an original writer.

Mácha is the first great poet of modern Czech literature and at the same time the first modern poet born in Bohemia. Neither Kollár nor Čelakovský shows much subjective introspection except in some of their love poems, and even in these their insight is not very deep. Čelakovský's philosophy in the second part of his *Hundred-leaved Rose* is quite bookish and lifeless. We see at once that his harmonious nature was far removed from doubts which often torment such souls as are extremely sensitive to inner vibrations of thought and feeling. Such was the soul of Mácha.

His career is short and pathetic. He was born in Prague as the son of poor parents, but was given a better education than most children born in poverty. At the university he studied philosophy, mathematics and law, passed examinations and in his twenty-sixth year went to the country town of Litoměřice in northern Bohemia to start work in the office of a lawyer. Not many weeks after his arrival a fire broke out in the town ; he helped to extinguish it, caught cold, and a few days later died from inflammation of the lungs—far from his family, forsaken and with an uneasy heart, when thinking of his betrothed whom he shortly intended to marry. This tragic end is still sadder if we consider that in the year 1836, only a few months before his death, he published the poem *May*, a great literary achievement.

His inclinations were romantic. He loved nature and solitude, visited old castles and ruins, was fond of travelling on foot to mountainous districts ; he also read romantic novels and poems of English, German and Polish authors. His mood was often melancholy ; he liked to think of death and the life after death ; but his mind was analytic and could not be easily satisfied with the desires and illusions of his heart. He loved his betrothed passionately although he saw the abyss between her treacherous and superficial soul, and his own ideal of true womanhood. These differences and incompatibilities influenced not only his disposition but also his philosophy and poetry. He often thought of the inevitable future, that dark night and still darker void which lay open like a yawning chasm before the eyes of his hero William on the night before his execution, when he reflected on what would come after ; and this was the picture which presented itself to the poet himself when he endeavoured to devise an acceptable solution to the problem of the relation of life to death. His reasoning power was too penetrating, his heart too honest to conceal from himself the conclusions at which he arrived. Being unable to reconcile the discrepancies, he could not attain any inner happiness; and the painful realities of his short life and sudden death did not allow him to derive any happy solution from elsewhere.

Like Pushkin and Lermontov in Russia Mácha also was called a Byronist, and we may say, with the same justice or injustice. It is right to consider him a Byronist but not in the sense that he was only a slavish imitator of Lord Byron. Being a great poet, he only adopted the external manner of Byron. Some of his plots and characters remind us of Byron's romantic tales in verse, like the *Giaur*, the *Corsair*, *Lara*, *Parisina*, or the *Prisoner of Chillon*. In this sense, his principal achievement, *May*, is a Byronic poem. It is the story of a man whom the poet calls William (Vilém), ' the dreadful lord of woods ', and of his love Jarmila who was seduced by his own father. On discovering this, William kills his father, and is then arrested, imprisoned and beheaded. A few years afterwards the poet comes on horseback to the hill where William was executed, sees his white skull on the torture-wheel and hears the rattling of his skeleton; an innkeeper gives him an account of the murderer's crime and death. And as if attracted by his ghastly narrative, he comes again after a longer time, just on the anniversary of the execution, looks at the skeleton in the moonshine, remembers his vanished youth, and deep melancholy steals into his heart.

If there was nothing more than this story and the reflexions of the imprisoned William, we could easily call Mácha's *May* an imitation. But there is great poetry in his descriptions of nature, and particularly in his images which express his thoughts and feelings ; and there is a musical language, too, such as no other Czech poet used before him and only very few after. These qualities, which we also find in his other poems and in his prose, constitute the unique excellence of his fragmentary work. They were his own, coming from his innermost being, and they secure him a place among those immortal poets who died before their power matured.

Of all his contemporaries, or those who would have become his contemporaries had he lived longer, BOŽENA NĚMCOVÁ (1820-1862) is perhaps the only Czech writer who possessed a creative power and originality approaching his own. She is the greatest poetess among Czech novelists. Although she happened to be born in Vienna, she spent her youth in north-eastern Bohemia, the home-country of her mother. There she was educated under the influence of her grandmother, a simple country woman who was the soul of all her early environment. Her folk-tales, customs and popular wisdom introduced her to an intimate knowledge of the peasants and their life, so that she could never forget them, even when she had to live in Prague. But this happiness in a beautiful district, near the country residence of a noble lady in whose service her father was employed as a groom, did not last long. At the age of seventeen she married a custom-house officer who was twice her age. He did not understand her higher interests; the frequent changes of residence from village to village did not contribute to her happiness, especially when the family and with it the financial troubles, increased. At last she had to support her four children in the direst straits, when her husband, a stubborn man and a Czech patriot, was dismissed by the Austrian authorities. After some time he was re-instated again but sent to Slovakia, while his family was living at Prague. Worn out with want and care, she died prematurely.

In Prague she had become acquainted with several authors who encouraged her literary tastes and induced her to write. She remembered the popular tales of her grandmother, had seen many popular customs in various parts of the country, and being supported by her memory or her notes, she collected and published, partly in books, partly in periodicals, Czech folk-tales and other folk-lore. Later on she added a collection of popular tales and some folk-lore from Slovakia.

She also wrote a few lyrical poems and several stories based on the experiences of her life. But all this work may be considered as preparatory to her novels. Her most creative period came when material difficulties caused her to contrast her position with the bygone happiness of her childhood. This moved her deeply, and under the influence of this emotion she wrote a prose idyll entitled *Grandmother*. The vanished world of her youth appeared in it with so much charm, so much simplicity and inner veracity that the book at once became a classic. It is a large-scale picture of country life in north-eastern Bohemia one hundred years ago. The grandmother is the central figure and her homely wisdom governs the small world around her.

Sentiment is the most important factor in this classical idyll as also in all the other works of Němcová, especially in her novel *Mountain-village*, and in her fairy tales which she adjusted partly to her own, partly to popular tastes. Yet the idyllic life which she portrays is not artificial—chiefly because there is no artificiality in the authoress herself. The world was pitiless to her, but she did not cherish hatred towards the world. She lived in misery, surrounded often by selfishness and narrowness of mind. But in her dreams she saw a better world and reproduced it with such warmth and directness that it acquired an enduring existence.

CHAPTER V

FROM THE NATIONAL REVIVAL TO THE NEW
POLITICAL INDEPENDENCE

2

Up to the end of the eighteenth century the
Slovaks had invariably used the Czech language
as their instrument of literary expression, though
we often find some local peculiarities in their
diction. The first writers who began to use the
Slovak dialect more systematically were some
Roman Catholic priests, such as the grammarian
and lexicographer Bernolák (1762-1813) or the
poet Jan Hollý (1785-1849). Their education
in the Hungarian seminaries brought them under
a stronger Magyar influence than the Protestants
who usually studied in Germany and always
considered the language of the Bible of Kralice as
their own, rejecting the innovation introduced
by their Roman Catholic countrymen. Kollár,
Šafařík, and other more or less important authors,
though Slovaks by birth, wrote in Czech. As
late as in the forties of the nineteenth century,
Ludevít Štúr (1815-1856), a Protestant, prepared
and carried through the literary separation of the

Slovaks, choosing the Middle-Slovak dialect as the basis of their literary language. His chief reason was political. He hoped—and his friends, who followed him, hoped too—that their native language would no longer be persecuted by the Magyars if, in their schools, books and periodicals, they used the dialect of their mountainous district instead of literary Czech, to which objection was taken. His expectations, however, were disappointed. The Magyars not only did not stop the persecution but increased their endeavours when the dualism of 1867 endowed them with all the political power in Hungary, and the Slovaks were delivered into their hands. Thus the great sacrifice, against which the Czechs, and many Slovaks as well, protested publicly, was quite useless. On the other hand, we cannot deny that the younger generation of the Slovak writers found it easier to express their ideas and feelings in their native dialect than in literary Czech because during the second half of the nineteenth century the Magyar authorities closed or Magyarised all the Slovak secondary schools and almost all the elementary schools. But the Slovak dialect was at least spoken near at hand, while the Czech literary dialect could be heard only beyond the political frontier, which circumstance was of vital importance in pre-war Hungary.

Since that time Czechoslovak literature has flown through a double channel. Its branches are fortunately so near each other that every educated Czech and every educated Slovak can follow them both without making special preparations in crossing from one to the other. In several cases—and Štúr himself may be remembered as one of them—both branches were connected by authors writing partly in Slovak, partly in Czech. And it is probable that such cases will be more numerous in the future now that the political frontier has disappeared.

In Bohemia a new generation arose at the end of the fifties, a generation which we might call modern in the true sense of this word, because its representatives brought modern ideas into Czech life and literature. The preceding decade was one of the darkest in the history of Austrian absolutism, and it is usually associated with the name of Bach, the chief minister of that time. Never afterwards, except in the first three years of the last war, were conditions in Austria so oppressive as in the fifties of the last century. It was not until after the disastrous defeat of the imperial army in Italy (1859) that a new attempt was made to introduce more liberal institutions. The new generation hated this reaction and declared war against it. In their political and literary views they were anti-Romantic, emphasising all that was in direct contact with life ; they preferred the actualities of their own age to all the splendours of the past ; they were individualists in many respects, but at the same time took great interest in public and especially social problems ; they were poets but also liked to communicate their convictions through the medium of journalism.   Though rejecting all romanticism, they could not sometimes escape romantic proclivities of their own, and therefore did not eliminate an involuntary admiration for similar features in the works of Byron, Heine, or Mácha. The latter poet was chosen by them as their spiritual protector.   They saw in him an uncommon individuality and a great creative force. When they published their first miscellany, representing them as a whole, they could not find a more suitable title than *May*, and they themselves are known as the Generation of May.

The most remarkable man among them was JAN NERUDA (1834-1891).   He was the son of a servant and his origin predestinated him to become a poet and journalist of democratic views. The general and literary education which he received at the University of his birthplace, Prague, was deepened by wide reading, and by his travels in Western and Southern Europe and to the near East.  His numerous volumes of collected humorous, descriptive, and critical essays, feuilletons and sketches, which were written mostly for the journal *Národní Listy*, testify to his unusual erudition in many branches of knowledge, to his wit and critical instinct.

His short stories, above all those of the *Malá strana*, i.e., of that part of Prague in which he was born, belong to the early examples of Czech realism. None of his contemporaries produced a book, containing such detailed pictures of the characteristic figures that peopled the streets of Prague about the middle of the nineteenth century. These prose-works, their brilliant *esprit* and tender-hearted humour, made him a favourite of the Czech public, who almost forgot that he was a poet, too, and a more eminent poet than his friend Hálek, whom they placed high above him. His poetry was, of course, not so spontaneous as Hálek's. His critical mind checked his fervour, his wit and sense of humour quenched his pathos. Thus his first book, the pessimistic *Flowers from a Church-yard*, passed almost unnoticed, and his next one, the *Book of Verses*, appeared eleven years later when the public already supposed his poetic resources to have been exhausted. But in the last dozen years of his life the solitary and infirm man persuaded the world that he possessed more originality and a deeper sensitiveness than certain other poets who had been rated much more highly.

His *Cosmic Songs* (1878) with meditative lyrics on the universe and its relation to man ; his *Ballads and Romances*, in which he expressed modern ideas and feelings in the traditional popular ballad form ; his *Simple Motives*, comprising his lyric diary in the course of the four seasons ; and his unfinished collection of reflective verses of strong patriotic character, called the *Songs of Good Friday* : will always form a constituent part of Czech poetry. And we must not forget his cycle of short lyric poems from his *Book of Verses* where he manifested his devotion to his mother with touching notes of tender affection.

His language is often that of everyday conversation, his words have the savour of homeliness ; and yet this simplicity of style does not mar the effect of his poems. Reading them, we do not think much of their form which is not very musical. They bear such marks of the strong personality of the poet himself, that we respond to what he says or what he feels without noticing his style. With him the style was indeed the man ; and as the man was great, he could not produce anything which was slovenly, even though it fell short of the agreeable polish of average verse.

We cannot say the same of his friends, Hálek and Heyduk. They are not so complex as Neruda, they have not so many ideas and such deep feelings ; but there is more fluency, more ease in their talents. Both of them are lyric poets above all, especially Heyduk. It is true that VÍTĚZSLAV HÁLEK (1835-1874) wrote dramas also, superficial and unsuccessful imitations of Shakespeare. He also produced several tales in verse of indifferent

merit in the style of Lord Byron ; but we do
not remember his name because of them.   More
important are his prose tales and a short novel
which he wrote in the last years of his life on
themes taken from the rustic conditions with
which he was well acquainted.  His strongest
chord was struck in his short lyric songs, published as a whole in the year of his death, under
the title *Amid Nature*.  It is true that their
philosophical meditations are not very profound, but we find in them some charming
descriptive passages of the Bohemian landscape
in spring and autumn, in the dewy morning and in
starry nights.  They are unaffected, melodious
expressions of a happy enthusiastic soul and an
attractive personality, who long remained a
favourite with the reading public.

The development of ADOLF HEYDUK (born in
1835, died 1923) was neither precocious nor
multiform.  He published his first collection
of poems at the same time as Neruda or Hálek,
but having added shortly afterwards two other
volumes, he ceased producing during the following years.  From the fifth decade of his life, however, he produced a profusion of lyrics and short
stories in verse for more than thirty years.  All
this time he lived in a country town of western
Bohemia near large forests and not far from the
mountains of the Šumava.  His mind was very
sensitive and whatever impressions he received

from natural phenomena, from birds and flowers, fields and whispering woods, he turned into a song. His art was unpremeditated and his tunes were almost as spontaneous as the bird-notes which he knew intimately and also introduced into his lyrics. He was a born singer ; the melodious elements of his poems surpass by far his ideas and imagination. Therefore the most valuable portions of his work are his songs or those narrative stanzas of his fairy-tale *Grandfather's Legacy* that celebrate the charm of love and song. Besides this, the most popular of his numerous books is a collection of lyric poems, entitled *Cymbal and Violin*, in which he gave his impressions of Slovakia and its sufferings under Magyar misrule.

The Generation of May is also represented by an important woman-writer whose real name was Johana Mužáková, but who printed her works under the pseudonym of KAROLINA SVĚTLÁ (1830-1899). She adopted it after having visited the birthplace of her husband, a village Světlá in the Ještěd Mountains in northern Bohemia. She was born in Prague and between these two places she divided her love and the scenes of her novels and stories. Her vigorous mind was deeply interested in social and religious problems, and her keen interest was sustained partly by her experiences among the peasants of the Ještěd Mountains, partly by the influence of the French authoress George Sand who was well-known in

Bohemia when Světlá was young. She met some uncommon men and women among the mountaineers, and her romantic imagination added what she did not find in reality. Thus, in her novels—*The Cross by the Stream* and *A Village Novel* are the best-known of them—she depicted a long series of men and women whose characters and actions were sometimes more personifications of her ideas than real types, but who, in spite of this, suggested to the future realists in Bohemia that among the common people might be found individuals of deep human and poetic interest. Moreover, she was one of the first woman-writers in Bohemia who devoted close thought to the destiny of their sex, and partly in her novels, partly in some essays, discussed the question of the equal rights of both sexes in social life.

In the first years of the seventies a new group of poets appeared on the stage of Czech literature, the members of which were known as *Lumírovci*, i.e., the contributors to the weekly *Lumír* which was given its name after a mythical bard. This periodical was founded in the fifties by Mikovec, after his death was edited, for a short time, by Hálek, then renewed by Neruda and shortly afterwards handed over to the representatives of the younger generation. Their talents and literary efforts were of a heterogeneous character, but they had a common desire : to raise Czech literature to the level of older and contemporary productions of the larger and independent European nations. Not all of them may be called literary cosmo-politans, but even those who preserved the home traditions more than Vrchlický or Zeyer, for instance, tried to widen the horizon of their less erudite countrymen by turning their attention to foreign poets. Not all of them had the possi-bility to be educated in Czech secondary schools, which began to be opened again in the sixties after the pressure of the official Germanisation had relaxed a little ; all of them, however, broke off intellectual contact with the Germans. They studied other foreign languages, and read French, Italian, English, Spanish, Russian or Polish poets in the originals. From Goethe they took the motto of ' world-literature ' and endeavoured to overtake their elders who, in their estimation, were advancing too slowly. Those whose cosmo-politan inclinations and interests were keener, made themselves acquainted with the past cultures of European and Asiatic nations and imported into Czech literature a large number of new motives, ideas and forms. No wonder that some of their contemporaries took an unfavourable view of their endeavours and rebuked them for preferring foreign civilisations to native products. A similar thing had happened with Mácha, or not so long before with Neruda, who also seemed, at least to the more conservative of their countrymen, to prefer foreign literary influences to the national Czech tradition.

The most typical figure among the poets of this group is JAROSLAV VRCHLICKÝ (1853-1912). When he died, he was not quite sixty years of age, and illness prevented him from composing anything during the last four years of his life, so that his literary work came to an end in his fifty-fifth year. Nevertheless he wrote such a mass of verse, original and translated, besides a large quantity of prose, that the literary output of his life was greater in volume than that of any other of the world's writers except Lope de Vega. He published about seventy volumes of original lyric and epic poetry, more than thirty dramas, fifteen volumes of prose-criticism, essays and stories, besides a small library of translations from Victor Hugo, Leconte de Lisle, Baudelaire and a long series of other French poets, from Dante (the whole of his poetical works), Petrarch, Ariosto (the whole of his 'Orlando Furioso'), Torquato Tasso (his 'Gerusaleme Liberata' and lyrical poems), Michel Angelo, Parini, Carducci, and some other Italian poets, from Calderon (fifteen dramas), Camoëns (his epic 'The Lusiad'), from Verdaguer, Byron, Shelley ('Prometheus Unbound' and a selection from his lyrics), from Tennyson, E. A. Poe, Whitman, Goethe (the whole of his 'Faust'), Schiller, Hamerling, Ibsen, Mickiewicz, from the Magyar poets Petöfi

and Arany, from the Persian poet Hâfiz (his
' Divan ') and from the Chinese ' Shi-King '—
besides several anthologies from Italian, French
and English modern poetry. This astounding
quantity of literary work—altogether about two
hundred and fifty volumes—was produced by a
man who was not merely a writer; who had to
work during the day as a private tutor or schoolmaster, as a secretary of the Technical College,
and later on as a Professor of modern literatures
in the Czech University of Prague ; who had a
family, too, was of sociable temperament and
liked to spend his evening hours among his friends.
It is no wonder that his mental abilities collapsed
at last and that he died spiritually before his
bodily death.

But up to the tragic moment when he felt
that he could not continue and had to stop for
ever, he preserved his poetic powers undiminished.
The last volume of his lyric poems, called very
significantly *The Sword of Damocles* and composed shortly before he was broken down by
illness, contains some of the finest verses he ever
wrote. There we also find a poem in which he
describes the Demon of restlessness that drives
him from one labour to another, without
interruption, without alleviation. He could
not help pouring out verses by day and night.
His facility of composition was astonishing ;
metre, rhyme, rhythm—all types of European

or Oriental strophes—he produced impromptu. The surface of his consciousness or subconsciousness was always receptive to the faintest movements of thought or feeling, to any sensations or impressions, to all philosophical systems, to all art and literature throughout the world. In this sense he was the greatest impressionist in the European literature of the last century. Whatever he perceived, all found an echo in his brain or heart, all was recreated for the outside world in his melodious verses and strophes. Of necessity his poems could not always be on an equally high level; his poetry did not always express adequately his ideas, or his ideas were not always worth being expressed in poetry. The basis of his human personality was not broad and deep enough to bear the immensely huge upper structure of his sentiments, reflections and artistic experiences. Had he been able to stop from time to time to meditate on his impressions and mentally digest them, he would not have written so many volumes, but certainly he would have created works of purer beauty than some of his books are; he would not have translated so many hundred thousand verses as he did, but would have probably produced some of the classical interpretations of great poetic works in the Czech language.

During his life he was sharply criticised by some of his countrymen, especially by those who saw his genius and regretted that he wasted it more than was necessary by changing its gold sometimes for silver and copper. But we must take him as he is. Many are his books, immense the variety of their subjects and forms : from a laconic aphorism conveying everyday wisdom up to the voluminous epic, *Bar Kochba*, in which he relates the struggle of the Jews against the power of Rome ; from the strenuous tunes of a love-song to the pathetic reflexions on life and death, on Greek gods and Christian anchorites, on Nature and the spirit of solitude ; from concise ballads to large poetic frescoes in which he depicts weighty moments in the development of mankind, calling them the *Fragments of an Epopee* ; from the simplest quatrains or couplets to the most exotic stanzas and artificial numbers ever used in Europe or Asia. These riches, if nothing else, testify to the creative energy of his genius. As yet no one has analysed and estimated them as a whole. Portions only have been critically examined and blemishes have been pointed out. But the future may do him justice after it has separated the dross from the gold and ascertained how much gold he did produce ; how he widened the horizon of Czech literature and raised its level ; and last, but not least, how he enriched and refined Czech poetic diction, preparing thus the advent of such brilliant poets as Sova or Březina.

His best friend and truest companion among the poets, JOSEF VÁCLAV SLÁDEK (1845-1912), passed away only two months before him, after a long and painful illness.   He, too, was a remarkable worker, especially if we consider the unfavourable circumstances under which he wrote. He was the son of a peasant and craftsman.   At the University of Prague he studied natural sciences, but when he finished the prescribed course, he went to the United States, learned English, lived as a trapper on the banks of the Lake Michigan, translated Longfellow's *Hiawatha*, travelled along the Mississippi from North to South, observed the country and the people, and conceived an enthusiasm for their freedom, so little of which he saw at home.   On his return to Bohemia he edited the *Lumír*, was appointed a teacher of English first in a Commercial College, then at the University, married, and from time to time published collections of his verses.   The lyrics contained in the first two volumes were rather melancholy, the chief sources of their sadness being his longing for home during his stay in America and the sudden death of his wife. Later on, when he found new happiness in his second marriage, his spiritual horizon brightened again, and a series of charming poems for children, besides several collections of more serious poems, resulted from this short period of happiness. But his autumn was early approaching and with it illness, suffering, and a new gloom.  Just at this time he undertook the greatest literary task of his life : the *translation of* the whole of *Shakespeare's works.*

The English dramatist had been very well known in Bohemia before him.  From the end of the eighteenth century his plays had been translated into Czech, and from about the middle of the nineteenth a complete translation of his dramatic works helped to bring him nearer to Czech readers as well as to create a Shakespearean tradition on the Czech stage.  Then Sládek, who had manifested his ability by his masterly translations from Longfellow, Bret Harte, Robert Burns, Coleridge, Byron, Keats, Rossetti, Tegnér, Mickiewicz and other American, English, Swedish, Norwegian, Polish, Russian, French, and Spanish poets and novelists, started with *The Taming of the Shrew* and *Macbeth,* and within two decades he had translated thirty-two of Shakespeare's dramas, leaving the rest to his successor Klášterský.  He himself thought it his principal literary achievement, and most of his contemporaries thought so too.  Many of them underrated his original production, his lyrical poems and tales in verse.  These seemed rather homely and unadorned to them in comparison with the verbal brilliance of his friend Vrchlický, and in fact, they are.  He disliked all superficial pomp in his poems, just as he disliked it in his private life.  But no other poet of his group—and among his elders not even Neruda, who stands nearest to him in this respect—could make his verses thrill with such warm and sincere emotion.

The third member of Vrchlický's circle, JULIUS ZEYER (1841-1901), was older than either of the other two, but he began to write and publish later than they—after he had passed his thirtieth year. At first it was not easy for him to express his ideas in the Czech language because his education had been mostly German. Like Mácha and Neruda he was born in Prague, but he was of mixed European and Oriental blood. His father, a wealthy carpenter, wished him to become his successor in business ; young Zeyer, however, preferred to study Virgil and then, at the University, modern and oriental languages without any definite plan for the future. Afterwards he went to Russia where he lived as a private tutor in an aristocratic family. From there he sent his first short story to the *Lumír*, but before it could be printed, the editors had to rewrite it and improve the Czech style in which it was written. When he returned home, after having spent some years in Petrograd and Southern Russia, his small inheritance provided him with sufficient means to live as a writer partly in Prague or in the country, partly in France or Italy, or wherever his literary tastes or his melancholy heart called him. Like some of his heroes he seldom felt quite happy. When abroad he longed for Bohemia, and when in Bohemia he was thinking of Greece or Spain, of Tunis or the Crimea. His romantic disposition, exclusive tastes and rather moderate success among his countrymen— at least in the first three quarters of his literary career—caused him to feel not quite at home in his democratic native country. He wrapped himself in solitude, surrounding himself with crosses, statues and other antiquities which he had brought from abroad, or burying himself in the study of foreign cultures and literatures, from Ireland eastward to Japan, from modern Paris back to Biblical times.

His productions are romantic and adventurous in character. Drawing from old French sources, he composed a large epic on Charlemagne and his times, *The Carolingian Epopee*; remembering the tales of his old nurse, he glorified the heroic age of his country in his collection of short epics entitled *Vyšehrad*; he wrote a novel, *Jan Maria Plojhar*, the hero of which is a modern Czech of his own type and mostly of his own views; he renovated a medieval legend, *The True Friendship of Amis and Amil*, and invented a story dealing with the religious and national problems of a young Slovak in modern Paris, *The House of a Drowning Star*; he took his figures and scenes from Spain, Provence, Italy (*From the Annals of Love*) and from Bohemia or Russia, from Old

Scandinavia and Old Palestine, from Erin and from China, or Nippon, from imaginary places and from the streets of the French or Italian capitals. But he was no realist and hated the naturalism which was held in such favour by his contemporaries. He did not endeavour to make his Chinamen Chinese to the last detail of their manners, or his Frenchmen French to the last buckle of their shoes. Their Chinese or French costumes concealed people who were akin to him, and who derived their ideas from his own thoughts and convictions. He was more concerned with his own spiritual adventures or problems than with the customs, manners and problems of past ages and far off countries. At the same time, however, his inclinations were too romantic to be contented with everyday life and common experiences. He selected only those elements which suited his inner style; he accommodated them to his own tastes, thus creating new values and new realities which were not of this world. And it was natural that the contemporary critics and reading public did not always appreciate him. But at the end of his life the new school of the so-called Decadents, with Jiří Karásek at their head, found their affinity in him. They called him the prince of poets, analysed his works and praised them above anything that had been produced by the older generation. Among his contemporaries he was the best stylist in the sense in which Dante Gabriel Rossetti and the Præraphaelites are considered as stylists. He placed art high above the realities of individual or national life. He will certainly have readers who will appreciate his books also in the future, but the numbers of those who regarded him as one of the greatest Czech poets have decreased considerably since his death twenty years ago.

For different reasons, but on the whole in a similar way, the latest Czech criticism does not consider SVATOPLUK ČECH (1846-1908) as the most remarkable Czech poet of the nineteenth century. Thirty years ago, however, it was the custom to name him and Vrchlický as the chief representatives of modern Czech poetry, and even to prefer him to Vrchlický as the more national of the two. His deep Slavonic feeling was the main cause of his vast popularity during his life. When he published the *Songs of a Slave* (1895) in which he gave a pathetic expression to his anger at the political despotism of the Austro-Germans, the Czechs became so enthusiastic that they elected him a deputy and wished to send him, a dreamer and the most modest of men that he was, as a political fighter to the parliament of Vienna. He wisely declined their proposal and, to avoid all declarations in his favour, went to Italy.

He, too, belonged for a time to the adherents of the *Lumír* and was one of the first editors of this periodical when Neruda and Hálek left it in the hands of the younger generation. But his inner inclinations always turned more to the East than to the West. In his childhood he had often heard his father reading the *Daughter of Sláva* by Kollár, especially its elegiac prologue ; as a young student he loved Byron's tales in verse, Lermontov and Pushkin. Both Kollár and Byron, and to some extent Mácha, influenced him in his youth. His tastes grew romantic, his cultural and political ideals became Slavonic, drawing their inspiration from Kollár's lofty doctrine. He wrote tales in verse and epics in the manner of Byron and Mácha, and imbued them with the Slavonic ideals of Kollár. At the time of the Franco-Prussian war his sympathies were centred on the French communists. Then he undertook a pilgrimage to the Caucasus which he closely connected in his mind with the names of Pushkin and Lermontov. And when, after his return, he founded, with his brother Vladimír, his own periodical *Květy* (Blossoms), he observed attentively the political and social movements and tendencies in contemporary Bohemia.

All these inner and outer experiences are mirrored in his poetical works : in his epics, such as *Europe*, in which he catches the last glimpses of the Commune at Paris, and *Slavia*, in which he tries to solve, in a symbolical way, the difficult problem of the antagonism between the Russians and the Poles ; or in his shorter tales in verse, such as the *Circassian*, which reflects his impressions from the Caucasian mountains; or in his collections of pathetic and eloquent lyrics, such as the *Morning Songs*, or the *New Songs*, or the *Songs of a Slave*, in which his social and national sentiments as the member of a subjugated people finds the most outspoken expression. If we add to these his epics for which he drew the subjects from Czech history (*The Adamites*, *Žižka*, *Václav z Michalovic*, and *Dagmar*), or from contemporary Czech life (*The Blacksmith of Lešetín*, *Václav Živsa*, *The Song-book of Jan Burian*), then his satirical poems *Hanuman*, *Cowslips*, or the *Truth*, his idylls *Snow*, or *In the Shade of the Lime-tree*, and a large number of tales in prose, descriptive sketches, reminiscences, and above all his very popular satirical novels, *Excursion of Mr. Brouček to the Moon*, and *Excursion of Mr. Brouček to the Fifteenth Century*, —we have enumerated at least the chief specimens of his ample literary production. Although he had courage enough to express his political or social convictions and defend the national cause, he was by no means aggressive. The idyllic propensities of his ancestors, the peasants, were deeply rooted in his character. He hated war, believing that justice might and should be done to everybody without bloodshed and persecution. It was on these pacific principles that he founded his views of the social order and the liberation of the Slavonic peoples in the future. Intuitively, however, he anticipated an inevitable struggle and wrote a most fervent prayer to God that victory might not be given to the oppressors. He did not live to see the struggle and take part in the victory.

In this respect fate was more favourable to ALOIS JIRÁSEK (born in 1851) who alone among the modern Czech writers has won popularity and his nation's love to the same degree as Svatopluk Čech. Jirásek is a novelist, and Czech history is the main source of his inspiration. He has had predecessors in Jan z Hvězdy, Chocholoušek, or Třebízský, and a true companion in Zikmund Winter, a master of detailed pictures of the sixteenth and seventeenth centuries. But none of them was so successful in depicting the spirit of the past of the Czech nation as Jirásek in his numerous historical novels : on the Hussite movement in the fourteenth and fifteenth centuries (*In the midst of the Streams*, or *Against the Whole World*) and the battles of the Hussite troops in Slovakia (*Brotherhood*), on the gloom which befell Bohemia in the first half of the eighteenth (*Darkness*) and the national revival at the beginning of the nineteenth centuries (*F. L. Věk*). Nobody else has contributed so much to the knowledge of Czech history among the common Czech people in the last forty years, and through this knowledge to the national self-consciousness. During the Great War his books were carried round the world in the knapsacks of the Czech legionaries, and were read in the trenches of Russia, France and Italy, in the forests of Siberia and on the transports on the Pacific ocean when they returned home. Thus Jirásek not only wrote on history, but also helped to make it. He was one of those who stood at the head of the Czech people. In the first half of April, 1918, when the German armies attacked the West front of the Allies with all their power and pressed them back, he composed and read a solemn oath at a meeting in Prague at which more than six thousand delegates from all the Czechoslovak countries and from Jugoslavia assembled. ' So we are standing here', he declared as a spokesman of his nation on that day, ' so we are standing here, firmly convinced of the ultimate victory of Justice, of the victory of Truth over Falsehood and Deceit. At the cross-roads of history, we swear by the glorious memory of our ancestors, before the eyes of the sorrow-stricken nation, over the graves of those who have fallen for the cause of liberty, to-day and for all eternity : we will hold out and will never give way! We will be faithful in all our work, struggles and sufferings, faithful unto death! We will hold out unto victory ! '

It is natural that a man, who feels the significance of the present time so deeply, understands and explains to his people also its past in such a way that it ceases to be but history and becomes a force which forms its future.

A deep national feeling pervades also the works of three among his contemporaries : the poetess Eliška Krásnohorská and the two Slovak poets, Hurban Vajanský and Hviezdoslav. Krásnohorská, whose real name is Eliška Pechová (born at Prague, 1847), is the most prominent among the Czech women who have used verse as their literary instrument. Besides several collections of lyrics and two shorter epics she also made some attempts at drama and wrote eight librettos to the operas of Bendl, Smetana, and Fibich. Although her bodily health has been rather weak for the greater part of her life, it has never affected her energetic spirit. A vigorous optimism is the main tenour of her lyrical poems from her earliest collection, *The May of Life*, down to her *Living String* and *Reminiscences* ; an optimism which perceives the difficult position of her people and sees the obstacles that check its political and cultural development, but in spite of this believes in a more favourable future and does not cease exhorting her countrymen to perseverance, racial self-consciousness and manliness. This patriotic tendency of her eloquent verses produces their strong didactic strain, too, and contributes to their being sometimes more rhetorical than poetic. Even her descriptive passages, e.g., in her best collection of lyrics, *From the Šumava*, suffer sometimes both from the want of imaginative sublimity and the easy flow of words. Accordingly the most successful of her poetic translations from foreign languages are those in which she can display the verbal qualities of her style. And the best of them are not the idyllic epos *Pan Tadeáš*, by Mickiewicz, though this is a remarkable achievement, or of the drama *Boris Godunov* and the shorter epics by Pushkin, but *Childe Harold's Pilgrimage*, by Lord Byron, whose eloquence found in Krásnohorská a congenial interpreter.

Her inborn energy did not stop before the problems of practical life. The Industrial School for Women at Prague which she helped to govern for many years, and the first secondary school (Gymnasium) for girls—first not only in Prague but also in the whole of Austria before Bohemia acquired her independence—a school which she founded under the name of ' Minerva ' and which is called now ' Krásnohorská,' testify to the many-sidedness of her interests, as well as to her organising talent.

Idealism combined with an untiring zeal characterises also the Slovak poet and novelist SVETOZÁR HURBAN VAJANSKÝ (1847-1916). As a son of the Slovak patriot and writer, Josef Miloslav Hurban, who supported, for some time, his friend Ludevít Štúr in his endeavours to separate the

Slovaks from Bohemia and Moravia, also in the sphere of language and literature, he imbibed a great deal of his stubborn Slovak patriotism and later separatism already in his youth. Nevertheless his own works indicate clearly how his poetic diction was formed under the direct influence of Svatopluk Čech, Heyduk and Vrchlický and how near it is to the literary language used at that time across the political boundaries. Having finished his education in Germany and his university studies at Bratislava and Budapest, he became a barrister and carried on his profession in various places of Slovakia for several years. But after he had returned from Bosnia, where he spent a few months during the Austrian occupation (1878), he gave up his profession and became a journalist in a small town which was then the centre of all the Slovak cultural hopes and aspirations. There he lived and worked for the only Slovak journal *Národnie Noviny* (National News) up to his death, leaving it from time to time to undertake a journey, or to be imprisoned by the Magyar authorities, for articles of which they did not approve.

His watchword was not that of *l'art pour l'art*, as he said himself in the preface to his collected works. The art he aimed at was that which might arouse the waning national sentiments of his people. This he tried to accomplish in his lyrics which he published in his journal or in the review *Slovenské Pohľady*, and also in three or four volumes. That entitled *From under the Yoke*, contains the largest number of poems, expressing his national sorrow and anger in pathetic, rhetorical verses and strophes. Otherwise his poetic production is not very manifold : personal impressions from the Tatra mountains or from the Adriatic and Dalmatia, occasional reflexions, some echoes of national folk-songs, here and there a short tale on historic, social or fantastic *themes*, or a fragment of a novel in verse—such are his chief topics and his usual forms. His limpid style, smooth rhythms and regular rhymes make his poems easy reading, but their want of higher æsthetic qualities does not stir our imagination.

Of a higher value are his novels and stories in which he depicted the contemporary Slovak society, i.e., not only of Slovaks in the true sense but also the Magyarised or Magyar officials, landed proprietors and Jews of Slovakia. As in his poems he indirectly admonished and encouraged his countrymen also in his prose, feeling deeply the national humiliation of his country and hearing everywhere its ' dying voice '. He could not always represent the characters and manners he observed around him without yielding to the patriotic tendency which was his foremost aim. With plain directness he portrayed the denationalised and selfish gentry, the cunning fraudulent

Jews who too willingly served the cause of Magyar tyranny, lawyers, doctors, schoolmasters and clergymen who acquired their education and very often their moral and political views in Magyar or German schools, villagers, peasants and shepherds whose passivity played into the hands of the governing classes. Being one of the leaders of its people and its public spokesman, he was confronted with the sad condition of his race every day and every hour. But he could not reproduce it always in its sadness because he did not wish to deprive his readers of all their hope and courage. He therefore altered and conventionalised his pictures, simplified or distorted his scenes and characters in order to accommodate them to his final purpose. In this respect he was inferior to the great Russian realists, who were his masters. Even his best novels, the *Withered Branch* and the *Root and Offshoots*, are not quite free from these blemishes. If we, however, consider the circumstances under which he worked, and recollect that the modern Slovak novel is chiefly his creation, we must credit him with being the best Slovak novelist in the second half of the nineteenth century.

Journalism, that affected Vajanský's work rather unfavourably, did not impede the literary activity of his younger contemporary HVIEZDOSLAV (1849-1921). His real name was Pavol Országh, and the family of which he came, belonged to the lower and poorer Slovak gentry in the mountainous district of Orava. The Magyar schools, to which he was sent by his parents, nearly deprived him of his national feeling and consciousness ; but under the influence of his mother, his former teacher, and the Slovak poet Matúška, who gave his people its national anthem, his disposition underwent a change, and he became a Slovak patriot.

Hviezdoslav, like Vajanský, became a barrister, but at the age of fifty he abandoned his profession, moved to his native place, brought up his brother's children, wrote verses, and arranged his collected works. He never was a politician in the usual sense of this word ; but the memorable year 1918 placed him among those who represented also the political aims and efforts of his people. In the spring of that year he took part in the festivities connected with the jubilee of the National Theatre at Prague, which symbolically prepared the independence of the Czechoslovak nation, and after the armistice he became a member of the first National Assembly in the capital of the new State.

His first volume of lyrics, his *Primroses*, were imbued with youthful pessimism, and that we discover, from time to time, also in his later books, in his *Twigs* or *Complaints*, gloomy thoughts preying on his mind and heart. But as a whole his lyrical poems bear witness to his manly courage and confidence, to his idealism and deep love of his country and nation. His *Psalms and Hymns* and his *Sonnets written in Blood* (1914-1915) are especially distinguished by these sentiments, expressed in fervent words of reflection or prayer.

Besides lyrics he produced a considerable number of epic poems. Biblical or historical stories and personages, and the everyday life of Slovak villages, form the main subjects of the smaller ones. Three of the epics surpass the rest, not only in length but also as impressive pictures of the people and nature in Orava. *The Gamekeeper's Wife* tells us the tragic story of the young and beautiful wife of a gamekeeper, how she kills the son of the lord, who is her husband's master, when he intrudes into their cottage to offer her his love, and how she expiates her crime by temporary madness; *Ežo Vlkolinský* and *Gábor Vlkolinský* depict in broad lines the life, manners and customs of the Slovak gentry and villagers throughout the year, their personal sorrows and family festivals.

He is less successful in his attempts at drama. From his youth he dreamed of the theatre, read classical dramas, and wrote several popular plays, but, living in a small country town he had very little opportunity of acquiring the experience necessary for the production of good drama. Hence his greatest work of this sort, the tragedy *Herod and Herodias*, is so ornate and exuberant that it is impossible to play it in its original form.

These works were published in four large volumes during his life.  Others remained in the obscurity of various periodicals—especially his *translations* from Shakespeare, Goethe, Schiller, Mickiewicz, Slowacki, Pushkin, Lermontov, Petöfi, Madách and Arany.  They give evidence of his endeavours to widen the literary horizon of his countrymen by introducing to them classical poems in Slovak garb, and of his resemblance, in this respect, to his contemporaries of the school of Jaroslav Vrchlický.

As an original poet he surpasses all others whom Slovakia has produced, though not even he can be acquitted of the reproof that diffusiveness and rhetoric sometimes spoil his higher qualities : his gift of vision and poetic expression which enables him to catch and fix evanescent glimpses of his native mountains ; his power to exhort his compatriots by verse and image at a period of dark oppression ; and, above all, his capacity for infusing new life into the poetic diction of his native dialect.

## CHAPTER VI

### FROM THE NATIONAL REVIVAL TO THE NEW
### POLITICAL INDEPENDENCE

3

AT the beginning of the eighties of the last century two important cultural events happened at Prague : the opening of the new National Theatre and the re-opening of the old Czech University— or, in other words, the dividing of the Czech University which was founded by King Charles IV in the fourteenth and Germanised by the Habsburgs in the eighteenth centuries, into a Czech and a German University. The National Theatre that was burnt down shortly after its opening and rebuilt in the following two years by public subscription, is a monument of modern Czech architecture, painting and sculpture. It may be termed the centre of modern Czech music ; for the great operas by Smetana, Dvořák, Fibich, and other Czech composers are not merely produced chiefly under its roof, but were also composed to be produced there, at least before other centres of music in Czechoslovakia were created. Up to this day, however, none of the Czech dramatists whose works have been played on the stage of the National Theatre can be said to be on a level with the genius of Bedřich Smetana.

The University, at any rate, influenced modern Czech scholarship and literature in a large measure. Under the leadership of TOMÁŠ G. MASARYK (born in 1850), who became a professor of philosophy immediately after the University had been divided, and of JAN GEBAUER (1838-1907), one of the greatest Czech philologists and the author of the monumental *Czech Grammar on Historical Principles*, a new movement, known as Realism, spread from there in Czech science, politics and literature. The Manuscript Struggles, i.e., the elaborate and complicated proofs that the Manuscripts of Králové Dvůr and Zelená Hora were forgeries, and, on the other hand, the arguments of their defenders resulted in strengthening the position of those young scholars who attacked the genuineness of the Manuscripts. But the realism developed further, until it gave an impulse to the foundation of a new political party which never possessed a large number of members, but having Professor Masaryk at its head, became a very important factor in the public life of the Czech nation.

Czech realism was a critical movement, and the inspiration and activity of Masaryk in particular were essentially critical. There is hardly any department of knowledge, so far as it attracted his attention and interest, in which he did not

10

manifest this quality. His first book, *Suicide*, which he published while a lecturer in the University of Vienna, before he came to Prague, may be called a criticism of social and religious life in modern Europe. In his later books, *The Czech Question, Our Present Crisis, Jan Hus*, and *Karel Havlíček*, he expounded and critically estimated the main features of the Czech religious reformation in its relation to the national revival, and of Czech politics and Czech programme in general. In his *Social Question* he critically investigated and ethically valued the philosophical foundations of modern socialistic doctrines, in particular of those of Karl Marx and his friend Engels ; while his largest work, the first two volumes of which were translated into English under the title *The Spirit of Russia*, is still the best critical account of the currents of Russian spiritual and social life during the nineteenth and in the first decade of the twentieth centuries. But also his other writings, his philosophical books and essays, his numerous contributions to journals and periodicals on literary, religious and social problems, his famous speeches in the parliament of Vienna, and above all, his vehement attacks upon the intrigues of the Austrian and Hungarian diplomatists against Serbia before the war, bear witness to his eminent critical abilities.

Criticism is usually repugnant to those to

whom it is applied, or whose cause it affects adversely. It creates enemies. And Masaryk had many enemies among his older contemporaries whose idols he demolished. For he was an iconoclast in his younger days, and those who perceived only this side of his public activities overlooked his merits as a teacher of the coming generation, as a politician, or as a religious thinker. His personality, however, was too strong and his convictions too deeply rooted in his mind and heart to be shaken by the blasts of public disfavour. It is true that he pulled down ruinous shrines or chapels where there were no saints and no gods, but he built greater things than he destroyed. He discouraged the belief in the Manuscripts but at the same time strengthened the trust of his countrymen in the work of the Czech religious reformers and the leaders of the national revival. Often he deplored the grandiloquent and sterile enthusiasm of the younger men, but he taught his pupils to work patiently even if nobody appreciated what they were doing. He often disapproved of the policy pursued by the Czech representatives in Vienna and was therefore suspected of being rather Austrian in his views; but when the time arrived no one did more than he to organise the nation and to recover its political independence. On his return to Prague as the first President of the Czechoslovak Republic everybody saw that his literary and educational work had been a preparation for his glorious achievements as a statesman, and those who disliked his 'negative' criticism began to understand its close connection with what they would call 'positive work'. But whether positive or negative, whether a teacher or a politician and statesman, whether a thinker or an organiser, whether a humanitarian or a fighter, Masaryk always was a moral personality first and foremost. Whatever he did or wrote proceeded from his innermost convictions and feelings. His acute, analytical reason, linked to a religious heart, shrank from all officialdom and detested indifferentism of whatever kind more intensely than open scepticism and disbelief. His moral and social fervour made him practically a socialist though he never belonged to a socialistic party, and in one of his important books, he impugned the philosophical basis of the chief socialistic doctrine. He did not preach to others what he would not undertake himself. His writings and his actions reveal a remarkable personality : a man of vigorous and versatile intellect, with a profound sympathy with those who suffer and are oppressed. This explains not only his resoluteness and moral courage, but also his influence on the younger generation before the war and his success after the tremendous struggle broke out. Modern Czech history is unthinkable without Masaryk and his great work.

He was, however, not the only man in Bohemia during the nineties who educated his countrymen by criticism and who made them aware of the various problems of the present day. The whole age was a critical one—so critical that some superficial observers saw nothing else in the contemporary literature than what they termed a destructive hypercriticism. Czech critics of that time were often dissatisfied with what they found at home, not because they always preferred foreign achievements to their own, but because they possessed higher, or at least more modern ideals of poetry and prose, of art and philosophy than the average of their fellow-countrymen and contemporaries. They studied foreign models in order to cultivate their own tastes ; they pointed to their real, or sometimes only presumed superiority, wishing to raise the level of literary production. But when they met a true poet or artist at home as was the case with Mácha and Neruda, with the painters Mánes and Aleš, or with the composer Smetana, they did not withhold their praise. Their criticism was more constructive than it seemed to be to the uninitiated.

The most prominent among them is F. X. Šalda (born in 1867), whose essays, partly collected in the books, *The Struggles for the Morrow* and *Soul and Work*, prepared the way in Bohemia for new conceptions of art and literature, and

created a new critical style. He is not a critic
in the usual sense, i.e., a man who carries out a
certain system of critical rules, of critical dogmas,
according to which he then accepts or rejects the
products of other writers. He declares in one of
his essays, which contains his critical confession,
that only such a spirit is entitled to criticise who,
having been born to admiration and worship,
has been disappointed in what he admired and
adored. True criticism is to him the most
heroic and honest form of scepticism—scepticism
whose only desire is to be refuted. Therefore
to be a critic means to suffer—the more so the
deeper the convictions from which his judgment
proceeds. A true critic does not criticise with his
reason only ; his whole being, his disposition and
polarity, his own destiny contribute to the
formation of his verdicts. There is no substantial
difference between a critic and a poet, in so far as
both are creators ; both must pass sentences which
are not just, both are passionate and therefore
not objective, both often violate their own dreams.
Their relation to art is quite personal, direct,
and must be acquired before each phenomenon
anew. Neither a poet, nor a true critic can
live on stock impressions, images or arguments.
Both of them must be susceptible to the highest
degree and must be full of inner potentialities.

A critic of such a kind is Šalda himself, uniting
in his person a poet, a novelist, a scholar, a stern

judge of art and literature. His drama, *The Hosts*, published quite recently, testifies to his ability to perceive and understand the budding of new social hopes, just as his early essays and criticisms gave evidence, thirty years ago, that he comprehended the philosophical positivism or artistic realism and naturalism. He never was a positivist or naturalist himself, nor can he be called a radical socialist or communist to-day; but his mind and critical personality were always pliant enough to follow every movement that ruffled the surface of contemporary art and literature—and not only to follow it, but also to master its doctrines, grasp its essential features, and by doing so to interpret the works of those who represented it. Thus he explained Taine beside Ruskin, Rousseau beside Flaubert and Zola, Shakespeare beside Ibsen and Huysmans, Masaryk beside Mácha and Březina, Aleš beside Munch, romanticists beside neo-classicists, individualists beside staunch supporters of collectivism, impressionists beside expressionists, obstinate sectarians beside stubborn Roman Catholics. It would be a pure eclecticism if he had treated them all at the same time, with the same gratification and zest. In reality he grappled with each of them, challenging them according to his own predispositions and inclinations at each particular period.

This passionate fighter cannot be an objective judge, and he does not wish to be one; he cannot be an objective creator of imaginative personages and actions as his great novel, *The Puppets and the Workers of God*, proves by a number of its figures, manifesting his own predilections or antipathies towards them more clearly than is usually the case with born epic and dramatic poets. In his novels or stories, however, and in his lyrics and critical essays alike, he is a true poet not merely as to his beautiful, imaginative language, but also by reason of the inspiration which streams from them and which fructified a large portion of modern Czech literature in its last phase.

Among his contemporaries probably no one underwent the influence of his writings and personality more strongly than his friend RUŽENA SVOBODOVÁ (1868-1920). Her early stories, novels and descriptive sketches, which she produced in the nineties, betray the realistic and especially the visual basis of her artistic talent. Her senses are alert and subtle, her attention quick and eager, her perceptions acute and accurate. She likes to depict nature in its changing moods, fresh colours and breezy draughts. She peoples her works with peculiar characters detected in remote towns and villages. She loves the Russians : Pushkin and Lermontov, Turgenyev, Gontcharov and Tolstoy, but especially Gogol and Dostoyevsky ; she does not, however, imitate them. Her realism is of a different kind. It supplies her mind with a large stock of impressions, experiences and ideas that are very useful as a source from which she draws the material for her figures, their manners, habits and oddities. But she dislikes the reality surrounding her heroines. And so do they, too, her young women and girls, who feel rather painfully the discrepancy between their sensitive natures and the frigid, apathetic world in which they have to live and which kills their illusions, destroying ultimately what is best in their beings.

These 'lonely souls' of her first books, the *Shipwrecked*, the *Overburdened Ear*, and *On Sandy Soil*, are followed by women of more complicated characters; her realistic or semi-realistic style slowly changes into a symbolical one. Her heroines become not only more self-conscious but also more active. Individuals ripen into types, representing the rising generation of women of the transition period, whose expanding intellects often contend with their sexual instincts. In most of her later books, in her *Sweethearts* and the *Black Foresters*, in her *Sacred Spring* and *After the Wedding Breakfast*, in her tales as well as in her largest novel, *The Garden of Irem*, we meet these beings of uncommon charm and very often of tragic destinies. Some of them are plain children of the country, others again come of aristocratic families; some live their idyllic existence amid the mountains, far from society, others again in the very centres of modern civilisation and culture;

some perish unredeemed, others pass through the afflictions of their sombre lives, finding at last their deliverance in love, or beauty, or some work done for their brothers and sisters. Love is generally the main-spring that urges them, but it is not the pleasure of love. They are mostly pure and austere, if not ascetic in their conception of love, which is to them rather a longing for spiritual greatness or some absolute beauty and good than a source of delight and enjoyment. This heroic desire governs their hearts and determines their destinies. It teaches them to overcome their disappointments and adversities by noble altruism and inner fortitude.

Such beings as these are not usually transcribed from everyday experience. They personify the aspirations of the authoress, her spiritual thirst, her social and artistic ardour. As types of modern womanhood they are shaped according to her own ideas and cultural ambitions, though also the external reality has partly contributed to their formation. They result from her capacity to translate her inner visions into poetic actuality. From this creative power also proceed her later style and diction. And it is natural that for this reason she is more successful in her condensed stories, resembling sometimes thrilling ballads in prose, than in her large novel in which she tries to depict, in a more realistic manner, a large number of personages, actions, places, and situations. She knew it herself and wished to rewrite it in a more compact form. But a premature death frustrated her intentions at the very beginning. And Death prevented her, too, from finishing *The Paradise*, a book of reminiscences, in which she drew an enchanting and slightly melancholy picture of her native place in southern Moravia and the early years of her life. She produced it as a sort of spiritual relief in her last months, when the misery of war and her strenuous work for those whom the war deprived of the most indispensable things, roused her mental energy, but at the same time exhausted her bodily strength.

Women have found an interpreter also in JOSEF SVATOPLUK MACHAR (born in 1864), one of the spokesmen of his generation and the most popular among its poets. He declared himself to be the offspring of Jan Neruda ; and there are some similarities between these two men— notably the fact that each in his own time and in his own way became what we might call the conscience of their nation. He often employed his literary gift in the service of public opinion, or oftener, perhaps, against it. In his poems, satires, epigrams, and especially in his polemical pamphlets and feuilletons, he not seldom opposed the current dogmas and popular beliefs, criticising Czech politics at home and in Vienna, Czech public affairs, Czech writers and literature. His caustic wit, his vast knowledge of persons and their weaknesses, his literary skill, and in particular, his clear, trenchant style made him not only a dangerous enemy but also a very readable and influential author. This unpopular popularity was heightened by his deep national, though by no means conventional feeling. He strongly loved his race and country, in spite of all their short-comings and blemishes ; but his love resembled that of a stubborn pedagogue who keeps to the old maxim : ' Spare the rod and spoil the child '. He often wounded the old-fashioned patriots who did not understand how a true-born Czech and a poet, living moreover among the slanderers and robbers of his people, could write such blasphemies as he wrote in his ill-renowned verses : ' I am a Czech as I could be a German, or a Greek, or a gipsy and negro, if I had been born elsewhere . . .' They forgot that immedi-ately after it the not less important part of his confession followed : ' My Czech nationality is a portion of my life which I feel not as a pleasure and delight, but as my vital, inborn duty. My country is but in my bosom and I shall not trim it at the command of others . . .; it will live in other souls when my grave is covered with grass —and if it dies in those, it will be dead and gone, as Kollár sang of old.'

His own heart overflowed sometimes with emotion but his sharp, relentless reason quenched his exuberant feelings. He reminds us in this respect also of his master Neruda, but his epigrams are more biting than those of Neruda, his invectives in verse and prose more violent. This acerbity arises partly—at least in his younger days which he revealed to us in his *Confessions of a Man of Letters*—from a hidden fountain of pessimism from which also his early lyrics, collected in his *Confiteor*, soaked their acrid taste. Later on, his pessimistic moods, originating probably in his unfavourable social position, changed considerably under the influence of his marriage; but they did not disappear altogether even from those poems in which the charm of womanhood captivated his attention. His 'lyrical dramas', *Here Should Roses Blossom* (1894), to which he added, twenty years later, as an inadequate appendix a similar book, *Those Whom Life Has Betrayed*, and his modern epic *Magdalen* (1894) belong certainly to his most poetic achievements. Particularly his lyrical dramas where he sings, in short epics of dramatic compression and lyric mellowness, the burden of womanhood in various stages of life and society : unfulfilled desires and unhappy experiences in marriage ; moments of the highest joy and years of resignation. As a protest against social conditions his epic *Magdalen*, with its quaint heroine and its cutting criticism of the middle class society in a Bohemian country town, may be linked with *The Warriors of God*, a satire, in which he, under the mask of modern Hussites, attacked the leading Czech politicians of that time, especially their eloquent tirades at home and their weak opportunism in Vienna.

Towards the end of the last century a deeper study of the antique world roused his intellectual curiosity and immensely widened his inner horizon. He started with Tacitus and under his influence he evoked some of the later Romans, one of whom, Valerius Asiaticus, dying by order of Messalina, in view of his beloved garden, he greeted symbolically as his spiritual brother. This, and half a dozen other lyric poems from the fragmentary collection *1893-1896*, formed a prelude to his future books, *Golgotha* and *The Poison from Judæa*, *In the Glow of the Hellenic Sun* and *The Pagan Flames*, *The Barbarians* and *The Apostles*, down to his latest collections, *They* and *He*. Except the first one, which is still of a mixed character, they form a cycle, called by the poet *The Conscience of the Ages*. In lyric or short epic poems of lyrical tinge he here surveys the development of mankind from China and ancient Greece through the Middle Ages and the Renaissance down to the French Revolution and Napoleon I. Historical events and typical personages alternate in them with moods and descriptions, revealing the charm of countries and places ; old myths and legends follow dramatic monologues in which the author has confined his conceptions of bygone times and human destinies ; large visions of great creative power are followed by simple scenes or stories in verse without much inspiration. Anti-Christian views, and enthusiasm for the pagan Greeks and especially Romans, who ' are now but a dream and a fairy tale in this our babbling and stupidly sage century ', form the predominant features of this cycle. The magnificent white bones of Rome and the decaying figure of her murderer and grave-digger are pictures that never vanish from his mind. They smoulder behind whatever other notions of European history he expresses during his long series of poems. Although his views are much more individual and less eclectic than those of Vrchlický in his *Fragments of an Epopee*, and although the seven books of his *Conscience* contain specimens of his best and most characteristic pieces, the future will possibly prefer some of his earlier or less ambitious works—some of his subjective lyrics, of his descriptive sketches, essays, reminiscences, and feuilletons. As a prose-writer he is one of the most lucid, vivid and matter of fact authors in Czech literature, being the greatest realist in the generation of the nineties and the most consistent rationalist. The colours of his verse are never dazzling, his images are rather homely, but concrete and plastic, being inseparable from his thought. But their simplicity is often extremely effective.

Of the same stock, but not quite of the same qualities, is his younger contemporary, the anonymous bard of the withering Silesian branch of his people, PETR BEZRUČ (born in 1867). Though he has published only one volume of lyrics and never acknowledged it under his proper name as his own, he cannot be overlooked even in the shortest survey of Czechoslovak literature if we keep in mind the racial character of his products. His *Silesian Songs* (1903, 1909) originated not so much in the individual sensations and emotions of the poet as in his clan consciousness, if we may term so simply the whole complex of his love for those places and people among whom he spent his youth, and his intense sympathy for all who suffer from social or national injustice ; of his presentiment that his nearest kinsmen in the black country of Eastern Silesia must before long inevitably perish as a Czech tribe, and his deep sense of personal responsibility—not for their present suffering and impending doom, but for the ignorance of those beyond the Silesian boundaries who leave his subjugated tribe in its deplorable state of helplessness. In some of his poems, resembling now rough sketches, now huge frescoes of visions, he introduces himself as a miner, digging under the earth, his eyes shot with bitterness and gall, his soul meditating on revenge ; or as a mad fiddler who has thrown away his mattock, grasped the fiddle of his grandfather and plays now on its only string, the string of those seventy thousand who are dying in the coal district between Ostrava and Těšín under the tyranny of the Germans and Poles ; or as a colossal, hideous phantom with a blood-stained cloak upon his shoulders, one eye burnt out by flame, one arm shattered by a boulder, with a miner's hammer in the other hand, and with German rats and Polish Jews gnawing at his neck and hips.   So looks, he says, so looks Peter Bezruč, born in the country of Těšín ; so will he stand erect for ages to come, touching the sky with his head—Peter Bezruč, the everlasting conscience of the Czechs, the hideous phantom and last bard of a people that perished.

Verses like these could only spring from a heart which had lost nearly all hopes that the social and national oppression might cease before it was too late. Very few of his songs and social ballads touch his private griefs ; a few of them contain brief glimpses of the nature and country folk under the mountain Lysá ; the most powerful, however, sing the common sorrow of the dying seventy thousand. They are sombre, but not sentimentally plaintive ; pathetic, but terse and pregnant to the last epithet ; lofty even in anger, and always rooted in reality.

The philosophical and literary movement of the nineties which began with criticism, and based its æsthetics on a penetrating observation of social and national life, spread in the younger generation rapidly; but as it spread it did not remain the same either in theory or in practice. New currents, coming partly from Western Europe, modified its tendencies. In fiction the great French and Russian realists or naturalists exerted their charm and influence also during the next decades, but the young poets, whose natural endowments and artistic inclinations differed from those of Machar, felt themselves hampered rather than inspired by their doctrines. A reaction against so-called objectivity set in. Instead of commonplace mortals the young 'symbolists' and 'decadents', as they were defined by contemporary critics, favoured individuals of exceptional character; they preferred dissecting their own hearts to the discussion of problems concerning the masses; and they rejected the coarser clay of every-day words, choosing instead of them expressions of finer shades and delicate colours. Poetic diction changed remarkably in their hands. It became richer, more sensitive, imaginative, and musical—so musical that in several cases their verses seek their equals in the whole of Czech poetry.

It is true that not all the poets, representing this phase of Czech literature possessed these qualities in the same degree or at the same time. Some of them died on the threshold of their development, or grew silent before they ripened. Others again found their inspiration now in

external phenomena, now in their inner con-
flicts—now in social struggles, now in philosophy.
Thus, the lyrics of such poets as Sova and
Březina bear traces of a series of stages through
which their individualities passed.

ANTONÍN SOVA, born in the same year and
month as Machar, began his literary career as
a realistic painter of his native district in southern
Bohemia, which engraved ineradicable traces
upon his memory before he left it for Prague.
His *Book of the First Promises*, in which he concen-
trated his early collections of lyrics, includes also
descriptive sketches and poetic pictures in the
style of François Coppée who was very popular in
Bohemia in the eighties of last century. But if
we read the first-fruits of his Muse carefully we
meet sometimes with verses which do not sound
like an echo of Coppée's Parnassian melodies.
They surpass them by vividness of tone and
sensitiveness of observation. Moreover, they
contain premonitions of his later social dreams and
aspirations. This is true also of his next book,
*Pity and Defiance*, the title of which suggests the
main sources from which his inspiration is to be
derived in future years. A solitary spirit wove these
poems amid literary and social struggles, far from
the pine-woods and fish-ponds of his childhood.

But before the visionary side of his character
gained the predominance in his poetry, and before
he could sing his new conceptions of humanity,

he had to create also a new language, a new verse
that would be more suitable to his purpose than
the diction of Coppée or that of Vrchlický.   He
accomplished this in his following books, in the
*Broken Soul*, and the *Assuaged Sorrows*.   Both of
them record the griefs which pierced his heart,
inciting it either to melancholy or to revolt.   The
*Broken Soul* is an epic of lyrical intonation, written
in a free form of blank verse or in short strophes
of irregular rhymes.   Not only the soul but also
the rhythm is broken.   The inner langour of the
young man, whose sad reminiscences of childhood
and youthful love are, together with the gloomy
moods of his maturity, the main subject-matter
of the narrative, could not be transmitted to the
reader in Parnassian regular lines.   The ' worm-
wood brew ' that fills the soul of the morbid hero,
and filled the heart of the poet, too, has affected
also his language.   But it did not enfeeble his
poetic vision or impair its delicacy.   On the contrary, the introspective morbidity that invaded the
young Czech literature of the nineties mostly
under French and Scandinavian influences contributed largely to the subtle perception and magic
of style we meet with in Sova's later books.   His
verse became nervous and capable of reflecting the
finest shades of impression, the most transient
flashes of feeling.   Its musical rhythms mirrored
driving clouds, struck passionate notes of pathos
and caught the impalpable dreams of an apostle

who saw in his mind the 'valley of a new Kingdom '.

Shelleyan sensitiveness, Shelleyan revolutionary tendencies, and a Shelleyan spirit of love for the human race pervade Sova's lyrics from his *Assuaged Sorrows* (1897) down to his *Bleeding Brotherhood* (1920). Some of his collections, as e.g., the first part of his book *We Shall Return Once Again* (1900), or the second half of the *Bleeding Brotherhood*, called *Morning and Evening Contemplations*, echo his moods in nature, sketching in dainty images the innumerable changes in woods and meadows, in the sky, on the surface of waters, and in his own heart, when his eyes rove over the country of his youth and his ears glean its sounds. Others again, and above all his *Lyrics of Love and Life*, reveal his innermost experiences, his trembling hopes, cruel disappointments and ' proud sufferings '—not directly, in passionate utterances and sharp accents, but in songs and lyrical ballads, woven, as it were, of music and moonlight.

His sensitive heart, often wounded to the quick, but never wholly dejected or resigned, is highly responsive also to the ordeals of others. After he has appeased his wrath and assuaged his sorrows, he is seized with a fervent desire to remove the burden that weighs upon his fellow men ; to serve them fraternally, to heal their wounded souls and console them with a message of kindness. He therefore leaves the solitary mountains of dreams and sensations, of personal griefs and revolts, and descends to the valley, from where he heard voices of ardent feeling, voices ' to the silent Sun '. He descends to the earth again to bring his brothers and sisters the message of a New Kingdom. It shall be a Kingdom of freedom and courage. The soul will be its ruler, a powerful Soul, glowing like a gigantic lamp with the light of supreme Reason and the force of the greatest of hearts. Its cities shall be built of thoughts, and their gates, temples and halls shall be open to all that they may converse with God and, approaching Him, understand the value of humanity. Of a new humanity which will probably yield many a barren blossom, but which will differ in its character from the old world that it leaves behind with its patriarchal customs, spiritual pettiness and moral decay.

These hopes and visions he then celebrates in his *Adventures of Courage*, a collection of lyrics in irregular strophes in which his apostolic ardour and poetic chiliasm attain their culmination. Though he dreamed of the earth as the scene of his New Kingdom and often returned to its fragrant clay and murmuring brooks, he has, in the meantime, ascended an airy summit again. Thus he descends, for the second time, to sensations and subjective feelings as the primary, inexhaustible source of poetic inspiration, and instead of meditating on the bright future of mankind in general, he turns his eyes to his own country and people. His books : *Three Chants of To-day and To-morrow, Struggles and Destinies, Harvest, The Songs of Home,* and the *Bleeding Brotherhood,* indicate the development of his patriotism during the last decade and a half—a development from austere criticism with political tendencies through the phase of a virile love and sound optimism down to his anxious cares during the war and his brave counsels when the fetters were breaking. It is natural that a man whose spirit has always understood so profoundly the grievances of the oppressed, and whose melodious voice has always sprung from the most humane heart, could never be a chauvinist—not even in his vehement rhetorical poem in which he protested, in 1897, against the brutal attack on his nation, by the German historian Theodor Mommsen. His patriotism resembles that of Shelley who chastised his country when seeing or feeling its faults, or what he considered to be faults, but to whom its poets and philosophers, its mountains and lakes, its rural lanes and fields were ties which could never be broken asunder. But Shelley died early and could not ripen to Sova's mellowness and wisdom. He could not yet perceive the ' smile of Eternity ' and pray in songs of thanksgiving and gratitude, as Sova does in his *Harvest* . . .

It is impossible to call attention to all the works he has produced, to all his collections of poems, to his short stories and his novels in which he depicts either the youthful dreams, aspirations and griefs of his generation, or the social and national problems of his country. In whatever he has written, he *is* a poet, an exquisite lyric poet first and foremost : not only in verse, but also in prose, in the flowing cadences of his periods, in the delicate bloom of his images, in the music of his lines. His imagery is as rich as the undulation of his rhythms ; the colours of his verse are vivid, and soft shadows flicker over his words.

OTAKAR BŘEZINA, whose real name is Václav Jebavý (born in 1868), like Sova passed through a period of realism though it seems sometimes that all connection with the world of reality has been eliminated from the poetical works by which he is known to his readers. Direct contact with large cities, with the centres of modern life and thought, was not necessary to this solitary sage and prophet, who learned foreign languages and through the medium of books became acquainted not merely with the poets, thinkers and scientists of the present day but also with ancient philosophers and medieval mystics—European and Asiastic alike. His mind soon transformed external phenomena into symbols behind which he descried more recondite truths and tried to reveal them also to others. For every moment, he says, explains to us the secrets of centuries, and the smile of beauty, dancing like flames above the hidden treasures of earth, points to those places where we have yet to seek. It is like the broad, mysterious smile of the ocean, dangerous to a solitary mariner ; its message, however, is as the mystic letter of the universe, sealed with stars, that cannot be broken ; a letter that cannot be opened even by the ethereal hands of the most powerful of spirits but which will one day be unsealed to all.

In his books he endeavours to unravel this mystery, stage by stage. *The Secret Distances*, his first collection of lyric poems, is the most subjective, most melancholy, most pessimistic of all. In it his private sorrows allied with the pessimism of Schopenhauer throw their shadows upon his inmost conceptions. It opens with a poem in which he implores the ' strength of ecstasies and dreams ' to send down a fiery shower upon the offering of his soul ; but even in this invocation we read lines from the elegiac song of his youth, of the harsh savour of poverty which he tasted, of the elusive phantoms he embraced in the cell of his spiritual monastery. In a beautiful poem which follows he tells of his dead mother, how she passed through life like a sorrowful penitent, plucking from the tree of time only fruits with ashen flavour. But these and other images which we may cull from the introductory poems express only a part of his early melancholy and pessimism. Sombre feeling and thinking characterises most of the lyrics contained in his book. In some of them his gloomy mood darkens into a premature longing for Death, in whose mirror he pursues his pale, bewildered thoughts, struggling along a wearisome road towards the dusk and polar nights.

They do not, however, reach those icy regions of everlasting silence. Here and there glimpses of light appear, and ultimately the poet discovers the first streaks of *Dawning in the West*, as he calls his second volume. But the dawning does not yet mean a bright day. His sun is still the ' black sun of death '—if not throughout, at least in those poems that are closely connected with his previous book. His reveries of love and earthly happiness are but illusions, persuading him of his loneliness and showing him, when he opens his eyes, that the whole of life is a dream which must be dreamed because a curse, the consequence of a ' secret guilt,' is walking like a shadow from hall to hall, and wherever it enters, ' desire winces and the triumphant voice of music is struck down to the lowliest octaves of mute agony '. Nobody can tell through how many souls of bygone generations it has already passed, on how many rosy smiles it has breathed its earthly chillness. But redemption approaches. Not with a new aspect of life, but with a new aspect of bodily death. The material prison of the soul blazes in flames, its burning beams crash and through the opening in the roof the heavens are glimmering. Death, though merely symbolical, brings the soul nearer to God. And the poet, who in his *Secret Distances* yearned in vain for ecstatic visions and suffered distress because he could not revive the earthly joys killed by his dreams, sings now a dithyrambic ' Morning Prayer ', certainly one of the greatest poems ever written. It is the glowing effusion of a spirit who has been roused from darkness to light, and appeals to the Highest for grace to serve as an implement in His hand, to ennoble the lives of his brothers and sisters, friends and enemies, and prepare their eyes for the transcendant glory they are unable to see. He implores Him to endow him with such a strength as might lift the eagle of his mystic vision up to His throne. There will this gigantic phantom bring the Earth in his fiery claws through the black clouds of night, there will he sit down at His feet and humbly expose his proud eyes, dazzled with excess of splendour, to the shafts of His glances.

This poem introduces a new phase in the mental drama of Březina. From his next book, the *Polar Winds* (1897), we gather that he has abandoned his moral solitude which caused his former sufferings. His eyes have penetrated beyond the veil of external phenomena and acquired the power of ' second sight ' which enables him to speak of things unseen and unheard

by common empiricists or impressionists.  In the
' ecstasy of love ' he wishes to sing to those who
have not yet left this shore of time that there are
no sorrows greater than their lost victories, and
no joys greater than the rapture of the gaze
which has been strengthened by Eternity.  His
' queen of hopes ', as he calls his own soul in one
of the poems, has visions of worlds that are burning low in ' blood-red dusks ', and of others that
are still waiting for their blossoms ;  but when she
awakens from her trance, she responds humbly
to the poor pleasures of Earth, turning away their
eyes that she might not see their tears.  But these
poor pleasures of his brethren and their tearful
eyes are not the chief object of his altruism.  He
brings them consolation, but seeing in his fellow-
men, whose vision is blurred, merely his humble
collaborators in the fields of spiritual redemption,
he summons them to drink the ' wine of the
strong ' produced by ' Sorrow and Loneliness '.
As he himself passed through distress and woe,
finding at last his way to the supreme Light, so
he imagines and wishes that also those who suffer
in the ' polar nights ' of spiritual blindness may
be seized by the winds of everlasting desire and
brought nearer to the ' equator ' where the mighty
Ruler resides.  Only such spirits as have hardened
their strength in trials can be redeemed.  For
God, too, suffers from the inadequacy of His
creation ;  God, too, realises His own dream,

approaching it 'with the anguish of love through the secret of ages'.

Upon this creation Březina fastens his thoughts in his fourth book, *The Temple Builders* (1899). It seems as though he had returned to his beginnings—to that time when he felt the sadness of life so intensely. But there is a great difference between his present and his previous relation to sorrow. He does not think of himself, but of others, and not merely of men, but also of animals, plants and inanimate matter. He perceives that suffering is a cosmic law, and that even the highest forms of life are founded on pain. Dark serpents of doubt steal into his heart, but soon his prophetic optimism drives them away. Looking at the surface of earth, transfigured by moonlight, he forgets the darkness which enwrapped it some hours earlier, and immediately sees before him a battlefield of bright, victorious spirits.

The loftiest aspect attained by his mystic optimism is in his last collection of lyrics, the *Hands* (1901). There he chants in dithyrambs his cosmic philosophy, his sublime conception of the cosmic brotherhood, of those myriads of living and dead beings that extend their hands as in a magical chain towards their brethren across continents and silent realms of all oceans. The 'clatter of mystical shackles' stirs his dreams, and he also hears, from time to time, the music of myriad hearts that are far removed one from the other ; but he believes that even madness and grief help to forge the chain which, having been grasped by the hands of higher beings, enfolds itself in another chain until all the worlds and stellar spaces are embraced. The vast majority of men are blind to the faint glimpses of the ' new morning '. Nevertheless the poet foresees one Man, into whom all the myriads have been welded, a redeemed One who will be a steersman of the spirit-earth, directing its course to the shores of the secrets of God. For the sake of this future One who will comprise the spiritual strength and harmony of all creation, of all the millions of ages and myriads of beings—past, present and future, their agonies and victories alike—human life is worth living. For the sake of him it is joyous to live, even if we conjure a vision, as Březina does in the concluding poem of his book, of the far off time when the ' delivered ' Earth will be extinguished and the mighty current of Eternity will roll on. . .

Besides these five books of lyrical poems Březina has published one volume of essays in prose (1903). Though his *Music of the Springs* was not designed as a whole beforehand, its eleven essays were composed in those years when he embodied his philosophy in his last three books of poetry, and for this reason form a parallel work to his dithyrambs, prayers and meditations in verse. Their colours cannot be always so glowing, nor their rhythms so enchanting as those of his strophes, whether these are rhymed and regular, or quite irregular and rhymeless.  But the music of their verbal cadences is exquisite, and lofty, though subtle is the music of their thoughts.  Whether he describes the plain beauty of the world, or emphasises the importance of ' second sight ' in art, whether he calls the ' highest righteousness ' one of the most mysterious lights by which God's unity burns into the human soul, or explains the difference between the labour for time and the labour for eternity, whether he speaks of the summits of mankind, or bends with love and sympathy towards the disinherited multitudes, condemned to toil in blazing Gehennas and sub-terranean darkness—he always displays a vast power of vision. His enormous imagination enables him to express what he sees, even in his mystical ecstasies, in a language that, as regards its richness and music, has no parallel in the whole of Czech poetry and very rarely finds its equal even in the greatest European literatures.

In spite of their exceptional character his work and personality have grown out of the soil of his own country. His profound interest in the social development and organisation of mankind, his intense religious feeling, his belief in the spiritual brotherhood of all men, the living and those ' who whisper in our thoughts and whose breath we feel like a vertigo in places where no one before us has ever stood ' have much in common with the ideas of the greatest representatives of the Czech people from Chelčický down to Masaryk.

\*     \*     \*     \*

In this brief survey it is not possible to dwell on all the lyric, epic or dramatic poets, on all the novelists, historians and critics who have adorned Czech literature although there are names among them which would deserve to be mentioned if this account were a little more detailed.* Its purpose, however, was to show that the unknown nation in Central Europe, whose literary development has here been sketched in rough outlines, has endeavoured, in spite of all hardships during the last three centuries, to obtain its spiritual freedom before it was able to arrive at its political independence ; and that it did obtain it, at least to a great extent, as one may see also from its literary production. In this way it prepared the revival of its national state. In the same way, one may hope, it will strive to preserve it.

* One of them, Karel Čapek, the young author of ' R.U.R.', has become famous in England since these pages were written. Indeed, Čapek is the only Czech writer besides President Masaryk who is generally known in Great Britain at present. It would unduly increase the bulk of this book, if an attempt were here made to discuss the work of Čapek, for such an attempt would naturally involve an account of other Czech authors whose merits are equally undisputed, but who have not been inserted in this Survey. Those readers who are specially interested in the recent development of Czech literature will find the subject ably dealt with in Dr. Arne Novák's article ' Czech Literature during and after the War ' (' The Slavonic Review ', No. 4, June, 1923).

# EXTRACTS

(In judging the choice of the following illustrative extracts, which are arranged chronologically, the comparatively small number of available translations should be taken into account. This applies particularly to prose, and here again, the selection was further restricted owing to the difficulty of finding short representative prose passages, complete in themselves. As regards the verse, it must be emphasised that there are several Czech poets, such as K. H. Mácha, J. V. Sládek, Jan Neruda, and Svatopluk Čech, who are as writers significant, but whose poems are seldom adapted for effective translation into English.)

P. Selver.

## PROSE

| | |
|---|---|
| Jan Hus | Letter from Constance |
| Petr Chelčický | Concerning War and Cities |
| Jan Amos Komenský (Comenius) | Bequest of the Dying Mother |

## VERSE

| | |
|---|---|
| Jan Kollár | The Daughter of Sláva (Prelude) |
| K. J. Erben | The Willow |

| | |
|---|---|
| Jan Neruda | To My Mother |
| Svatopluk Čech | Our Native Tongue |
| Jaroslav Vrchlický | Adagio |
| „          „ | Eclogue IV |
| „          „ | The Graveyard in the Song |
| „          „ | Melancholy Serenade XXII |
| „          „ | Marco Polo |
| Antonín Sova | On the Hill Side |
| „          „ | To Theodor Mommsen |
| „          „ | Yellow Flowers |
| „          „ | O, that a Joy might come . . . |
| „          „ | Eternal Unrest |
| „          „ | The Morning Wind |
| J. S. Machar | October Sonnet |
| „          „ | On Golgotha |
| „          „ | Tractate on Patriotism |
| „          „ | Shakespeare |
| „          „ | Galileo with Milton at Torre de Gallo |
| „          „ | Cromwell at the Corpse of Charles I |
| Petr Bezruč | Kyjov |
| „          „ | Ostrava |
| „          „ | I am the first of the Těšín people . . . |
| Otakar Březina | Legend of Secret Guilt |
| „          „ | Pure Morning |
| „          „ | Responses |
| Karel Toman | Old Autumn Allegory |
| „          „ | The Sun-Dial |

# JAN HUS

## Letter from Constance

'10th June, 1415.

'Master Jan Hus, a servant of God in hope, unto all faithful Czechs who love and will love the Lord God, he uttereth his desire that the Lord God may vouchsafe it unto them to prevail in His grace unto their end, and to prevail in heavenly joy for ever and ever. Amen. Ye faithful and ye in God's grace, rich and poor, I entreat and admonish you to hearken unto the Lord God, to extol His word, and gladly to hear and fulfil it. I entreat you, as touching the truth of God, the which I did write from the law of God, and did preach and write from the utterances of the saints, that ye cleave fast to it. I likewise entreat any whosoever heard from me in my preaching or privily, aught against the truth of God, or if I did anywhere write any such thing—the which, in God's name, I trust is not—that he keep not to it. I likewise entreat any who beheld in me wanton usage in talking or in deeds, that he keep not to them, but that for my sake he ask God to vouchsafe me forgiveness. I entreat you to beware of the crafty, concerning whom the Saviour saith that they are in sheep's clothing, but

within are ravening wolves. I entreat the lords
to show mercy unto the poor, and to be righteous
towards them. I entreat citizens to conduct their
trade righteously. I entreat artizans to perform
their labour and enjoy it righteously. I entreat
servants to serve their masters and mistresses
faithfully. I entreat teachers that, leading godly
lives, they may instruct their pupils faithfully :
foremost, in order that they may love God, that
they may study for His praise and for the weal
of the community and for their own salvation :
but not for covetousness or for worldly glorifi-
cation. I entreat students and other pupils to
hearken unto their masters and to follow them in
what is good, and to learn diligently for God's
praise and for the salvation of themselves and
others. I entreat all in common to render thanks
unto these lords : Lord Venceslas of Dubá, also
of Leština, Lord John of Chlum, Lord Henry of
Plumlov, Lord William Zajíc, Lord Myšek,
and other lords of Bohemia and Moravia, and the
faithful lords of the Polish kingdom, and to be
grateful to their endeavour, that they many a
time stood out against the whole council, both
testifying and replying for my liberation, and
especially regarding Lord Venceslas of Dubá and
Lord John of Chlum, that ye believe what they
shall declare ; for they were in the council when
I gave answer, for several days ; they know which
of the Czechs and in what manner bore much and

unmeet witness against me, in what manner I
gave answer, what they asked of me.  I likewise
entreat you to pray the Lord God on behalf of
his Royal Grace, King of Rome and Bohemia,
and on behalf of his Queen, and on behalf of the
lords, that the merciful Lord God may continue
with them and with you in His mercy, now and
hereafter in eternal joy.   Amen.

' I have written this letter to you in prison
in chains, awaiting on the morrow to be
condemned to death, having full hope in God,
that I may not swerve from the truth of God,
and that I may not disavow what the false
witnesses have witnessed against me as errors.
In what gracious manner the Lord God acteth
unto me, and is with me amid sore temptations,
ye shall know when we meet in God's presence in
joy with His good help.  Concerning Master
Jerome, my beloved comrade, I do hear naught
save that he is in heavy duress, awaiting death even
as I, and this for his faith, the which he staunchly
displayed unto the Czechs.  And the Czechs,
those who were our most cruel enemies, delivered
us unto other enemies, unto their power and
duress.  I entreat you to pray God for them.
Likewise do I entreat you, more especially the men
of Prague, to show your favour unto Bethlehem,
as long as the Lord God may vouchsafe them to
preach the Word of God therein.   I hope in the
Lord God that He keep this place after His will,

and accomplish therein greater profit through others than He did accomplish through me with my shortcomings. I likewise entreat you to love one another, to suffer not the good to be oppressed by violence, and to grant truth unto all.

'Written at night on the Monday before St. Vitus' day '.

## PETR CHELČICKÝ

### Concerning War and Cities

'Thereupon the Saviour manifesteth the reason wherefore this great gift shall be on earth, and saith that it is for the mingling of the sound of the sea and the billows thereof. By the unquiet sea is signified sometimes a multitude of evil men, and sometimes a particular single one, even as saith the Lord God : " Unkind as the restless sea, which cannot be quieted ". This sound of the cruel sea and of the billows thereof our Czech land hath suffered much ; for well-nigh all the lands round about rose up against it from dissension in faith, so that the sound of those waves could be heard almost throughout the world. Also the raging of this sea can be, and oftentimes is wont to be, over earthly things ; for them doth the one party ever wage war against the other, desiring to exalt themselves above the others and to be their betters, and therefore do they wrangle and seize upon each other's possessions, upon men and honour, and therefore do they buffet one the other, burn one another, shed blood. Likewise also other sinful folk, like the sea unquiet and unquelled in evil, who are stirred by devils to unrest, that ever evil may go against evil, as

waves of the sea against other waves, quarrel against quarrel, pride against pride, hardship against hardship—in one place they have slain one another, in another place robbed one another, in another place challenged one another, as desiring to slay or rob one another. And thus is the most mournful sound of this sea to be heard. And amid all the storm of this sea is temptation uttered unto the servants of Christ. Even as spake the Lord, saying: *When ye shall hear of wars and quarrels, fear not, for this sea shall not overwhelm you with its waves, neither shall a hair of your head perish: if ye abide in me, my peace shall abide in you, and the storm of the sea shall pass by you.* And all these things, the which Christ here sayeth, do constrain us to hold ourselves in readiness, that we may be worthy of His coming.'
*From the Postilla* (1434).

## JAN AMOS KOMENSKÝ (COMENIUS)

### From the 'Bequest of the Dying Mother of the Unity of Brethren' (1650)

'Thee, Czech and Moravian nation, beloved country, I cannot forget now that my parting from thee is over, but foremost in returning to thee, I make thee successor and foremost heir of my treasures, which the Lord entrusted unto me, after the example of sundry rich Roman citizens and neighbouring kings who, when dying, appointed the community of Rome, which held sway over a great span of the earth, as inheritor of their possessions. I, too, believe before God that after the passing of the storms of wrath, brought down upon our heads by our sins, the rule over thine own possessions shall return to thee again, O Czech people! And for this hope do I make thee inheritor of everything not only all that I have inherited from my forefathers, and have preserved notwithstanding the troublous and grievous times, but also whatever increase I have received in any good work through the labour of my sons and the blessing of God, this all do I wholly bequeath and deliver to thee, and more especially :

'In the first place, love for the pure truth of God, the which to us before other nations the Lord first began to manifest by the service of our master—Jan Hus, and the which he with his fellow-worker and many other faithful Czechs, sealed with his blood, and from which the Antichrist by his guile at the Council of Basle led thee away for that time and thereafter by warlike and cruel power, yet have I with my sons, who desired to follow the light, hitherto striven to cleave fast to it.    Thine is this heritage, bestowed upon thee before other nations, O beloved country.  Take possession of thine own rights again, as thine own, when the Lord showeth mercy unto thee, and the Lord, thy Saviour, restoreth a pathway unto his truth.

'Secondly, I command unto thee a zealous desire for an even fuller and clearer understanding of this same truth of God, that, knowing the Lord, thou endeavour to recognise him more abundantly.  And whereas the Lord enjoined that the Holy Scriptures should be searched, I bequeath unto thee as a heritage the Book of God, the Holy Bible, which my sons did render from the original tongues (in which God ordained it to be written) into Czech with great diligence (sundry learned men spending unto fifteen years upon this labour), and the Lord God so blessed it, that few there are of nations yet which have heard the prophets and apostles speaking so faithfully, aptly and clearly in their own tongue. Take possession of this therefore as thine own jewel, beloved country, and employ this for the glory of God and thyself in good upbringing. And although copies of this Book of God were burnt by enemies, wherever they could lay hands on them, yet by the mercy of the same God, who ordered the Books of Jeremiah, torn up and burnt by the ungodly Jehoiakim, to be written anew, and the law of God, torn up and burnt by Antiochus the tyrant, soon afterwards, arousing the godly Ptolemy, caused to be rendered in the Greek tongue and conveyed to the knowledge of other nations, so unto thee shall this book of God be preserved, be sure and doubt not.

'Thirdly, I do commend especially also love for the ordinances of the Church and this beloved doctrine (which should and must be among the children of God), that thereafter ye may count Christ not only as a prophet in the pulpit, not only as a priest and bishop by the altar, but also as a King with throne and sceptre to pass judgment upon the disobedient. Now, what the Lord revealed unto me in his grace, that have I not hidden; it hath been brought unto the light. Do thou use this also, beloved country, for thine own good, either as has been done by me, or as may be discovered from the Holy Scriptures to be the most edifying way and after the example of the early apostolic Church! for to build upon old foundations, whenever the Temple of God is renewed, this is the safest.

'Fourthly, I do impart zeal in serving the Lord God and in serving Him with single endeavour. What I have yearned for from my beginnings, that the memorials of my forefathers and the history written by Jan Lasicius concerning my affairs, do testify. This indeed could I myself not fully use, save that in the year 1575 I joined in common with my nation of both confessions, and in the year 1610 with the common consistory; but may God grant in his mercy (the which desire I will seal either with my life or my death, even as the Lord may command) that the third union may be the most perfect, a union of all the remainders of my children with all other remainders whatsoever of faithful Czechs, that the branch of Judah and the branch of Ephraim may be one branch in the hand of God, when our scattered bones are gathered together again, and are endued with flesh and skin and filled with the spirit of life by the Almighty Lord, unto whom nothing is impossible.

'Fifthly, I do impart also unto thee and thy sons eagerness in the polishing, cleansing, and fostering of our dear and beloved native language ; wherein the devotion of my sons was known in bygone times, when by the more understanding persons it hath been said that there was no better Czech than that in use among the Brethren and in their books. But some there are now who have applied themselves thereunto even more diligently, also those driven forth from their country, that by the preparing of useful books and such as are written with a more cultivated pen than was previously the wont, they might help thy sons the more easily to attain all manner of noble comeliness in their deeds and speech, in wisdom and eloquence, a happy recompense for the desolation now ensuing, until the Lord may bring about times of amendment. Whatsoever then of this may be found, of old books or new, this receiving from my sons, take as thine own for such as shall seem best to thee.

'Sixthly, I bequeath to thee a better, more diligent and successful upbringing of youth than heretofore. This have I overlooked, entrusting myself to foreigners, who rendered my sons wanton and corrupt. If it had pleased God to restore me to more placid times, I would seek to make amends for this; but losing hope for myself, I entreat thee, beloved country, most importunately, that thou amend it. Divers of my sons have laboured likewise in this matter, and have prepared a method for the better upbringing of youth, the which other nations, without regard to religion, have begun to take in hand. But unto thee foremost it appertaineth, and when the time cometh, my sons, neglect not thine heritage, the which they are removing from thee.

In short, all my remains, as ashes after my burning, unto thee, beloved country, do I commend, that thou therefrom may prepare lye for the cleansing of thy children from their stains; even as the Lord made me in my beginnings, by raising me and my children out of the ashes of Hus.

'But what more is there to say? The time is coming for me to cease and to bid you farewell, beloved country! But what then? Even as the patriarch Jacob, upon his death-bed bidding his sons farewell, gave unto them his blessing; even as Moses, departing from his people: from whose lips I taking the words, unto thee, O Czech nation, bidding thee farewell, utter a blessing from the Lord thy God, that thou above all be and remain a fruitful bough, a fruitful bough by a well, whose branches run over the wall. Notwithstanding that they have filled thee with bitterness and have shot arrows at thee, the archers holding thee in secret hatred, yet may thy bow abide in strength, and may the arms of thy hands be strengthened from the hands of the mighty Jacob, from the powerful God, whom thy fathers served, who helpeth thee, and from the Almighty, who blesseth thee with the heavenly blessing from above, with the blessing of the deep-lying abyss, with the blessing of the breast and body. May my blessing be stronger with thee than the blessing of my forefathers, even unto the regions of the eternal hills.

' Be of good cheer, O nation consecrated unto God ; perish not. May thy men be without number. Bless, O Lord, their exploits, and may the toil of their hands be well pleasing unto thee ! Shatter the loins of their enemies, and of those who hate them, that they rise no more ! May thy time come, that the nations may say : " Blessed art thou, O Israel ; who is like unto thee, O people saved by the Lord, who is the shield of thy help and the sword of thine excellency ? Assuredly shall thine enemies be abased, that thou shalt tread upon their high places.

'"Thine, O Lord, is the salvation, and upon the people be Thy blessing, Selah." '

13

## JAN KOLLÁR
### The Daughter of Sláva
###### PRELUDE

HERE lies the country, alas, before my tear-laden
 glances,
  Once 'twas the cradle, but now—now 'tis the
  tomb of my race ;
Check thou thy steps, for the places are sacred,
  wherever thou turnest.
  Son of the Tatra arise, cast to the heavens thy
  gaze,
Or to the mighty old oak, that stands there yonder,
  incline thee,
  Holding its own against treacherous time,
  till to-day.
Ah, but more evil than time, is the man, who a
  sceptre of iron,
  Slavia, on thy neck, here in these lands has
  imposed ;
Worse than savage encounters and fiercer than fire
  and than thunder—
  He who in frenzy blind covers his kindred with
  shame.
O ye years of the past that as night are lying
  around me,
  O my country, thou art image of glory and
  shame ;

From the treacherous Elbe o'er the plain to the
   Vistula faithless,
From the Danube until Baltic's insatiate foam,
Where the mellifluous tongue of the sturdy Slavs
   once resounded,
Now it, alas ! is still, silenced by onslaughts of
   hate.
Who has committed this theft that cries for
   vengeance to heaven ?
Who has upon one race outraged the whole of
   mankind ?
Blush thou for shame, O envious Teuton, the
   neighbour of Sláva,
Many such sins have thine hands often
   committed of old.
Ne'er has an enemy yet shed blood—or ink—so
   profusely,
As by the German was shed, compassing
   Sláva's decay ;
Worthy of freedom is only he who values all
   freedom,
He who puts captives in bonds—he is a captive
   himself.

  .  .  .  .

Far to the right I gaze, to the left I searchingly
   turn me,
But 'tis in vain that my eye Sláva in Slavia
   seeks.
Tell me, thou tree, their temple of nature, under
   whose shadow

They to primæval gods offerings formerly
    burnt,
Where are these nations, and where are their
    princes and where are their cities,
They who the first in the North called into
    being this life ?
They taught the use of sails and oars to indigent
    Europe,
Taught how to sail o'er the sea, passing to
    bountiful shores.
Out of the ore-laden depths they dug the metals
    concealed there,
More from respect for the gods rather than
    profit to men ;
They taught the farmer to till the bosom of
    Earth with the plough-share,
So that the lands that were bare yielded the
    golden-hued corn.
They by the peaceful paths, the lime-tree sacred
    to Sláva,
Planted and scattered around fragrance and
    shadowy rest.

.    .    .    .    .

Where in marble arose the halls of the thunderer
    Perun,
Now from the ruins distress shelter for
    cattle has made ;
Where to the heavens uprose the old-famed towers
    of Arkona,

Yonder the stranger's foot tramples the
  fragments to dust.
There they bewail the ruins of Retra's temples,
  the famous,
  Where they arose now dig lizard and serpent
  their nest.
Son of the Sláva who comes from this land to visit
  his brother,
  Is to his brother unknown, presses not warmly
  his hand ;
Strange is his language that comes from lips and
  from countenance Slavic,
  Countenance seemingly Slav sadly the hearing
  belies.
For on her sons right deeply has Sláva imprinted
  her tokens,
  Nor can the place or the time ever their
  traces erase ;
Just as two rivers whose waters a single bed has
  united,
  Still for long on the way parted their colours
  remain.
So by violent strife are these nations confusedly
  mingled,
  Yet does their nature till now visibly sundered
  remain.
But have degenerate sons heaped often upon their
  own mother
  Curses, and yet in their guilt cringed to the
  step-mother's lash ;

They in their nature are neither Slavic nor
    Teuton, but bat-like,
    Half of the nature of one, half of the other
    possess.

       .     .     .     .

Forest, stream, town and village unwilling their
    titles Slavonic
    Altered; the form but remains. Spirit of
    Sláva is gone.
O who will come, these graves from a living
    dream to awaken ?
    Who will the rightful heir back to his
    country restore ?

       .     .     .     .

Now there are none remaining; the boorish
    countryman's plough-share,
    Crashing destructively on, breaks up the
    warriors' bones ;
Wroth at the worthlessness of two generations,
    their shadows
    Haunt the dim mist of decay, uttering cries
    of lament.
Uttering cries of lament that Fortune relentless
    continues,
    Letting their grandsons' blood either decay
    or be changed ;
Coldly in sooth would beat the heart of a man
    for his nation,

If he would shed no tears here, even as o'er
    his love's bones.
Ah, but be silent, O grief, serenely beholding the
    future,
    Scatter with eye like the sun thoughts that
    arose in a cloud.
Greatest of evils it is, in misfortune to wrangle
    with evil,
    He who assuages by deeds anger of heaven
    does best.
Not from a troubled eye springs hope, but from
    hands that are active,
    Thus, and thus only, can now evil be turned
    into good.
Only the man, but not mankind can stray on the
    journey,
    Oft the confusion of some favours the rest as
    a whole.
Time changes all, and by time is truth to victory
    guided,
    What in their error the years planned in a
    day is o'erthrown,

            *The Daughter of Sláva* (1824).

K. J. ERBEN

The Willow

In the morn he sat at meat;
Thus his youthful spouse did greet:

" Mistress mine, thou mistress dear,
Thou in all things wert sincere.

Thou in all things wert sincere,—
One thing ne'er thou let'st me hear,

We have now two years been wed,
Only one thing brings me dread.

Mistress mine, O mistress blest,
With what slumber dost thou rest ?

In the evening fresh and bright,
Like a corpse thou art at night.

Naught has sounded, naught has stirred,
Nor is trace of breathing heard.

Filled with coldness is thy frame,
E'en as if to dust it came.

Nor doth rouse thee from thy sleeping
Our young child, with bitter weeping.

Mistress mine, thou wife of gold,
Doth some sickness thee enfold ?

If by sickness thou'rt dismayed,
Let wise counsel be thine aid.

Many herbs are in the field,
Thou perchance by one art healed.

But if herbs can naught avail,
A potent spell can never fail.

Clouds to a potent spell will yield,
That ships in the raging storm can shield.

A potent spell o'er fire holds sway,
Rocks can shatter, dragons slay.

A gleaming star from heaven can rend,
A potent spell thy weal can send."

" O husband mine, so dear to me,
Let no vain word trouble thee.

" What was fated at my birth,
To no balm will yield on earth.

What has been decreed by fate,
At man's word will not abate.

Tho' lifeless on my bed I lie,
Ever 'neath God's might am I.

I am ever 'neath God's might,
Who protects me night by night.

Tho' I sleep as dead, at morn
My spirit back to me is borne.

I rise at morn from weakness freed,
For 'twas thus by God decreed."

Wife, these words of thine are naught,
For thy husband guards his thought.

At a fire an aged soul
Water pours from bowl to bowl.

Cauldrons twelve stand in a row,
The husband for her aid doth go.

" Mother, hear ! thy skill is great,
Know'st what each has to await.

Know'st how plague comes into being,
Where the Maid of Death is fleeing.

Tell me, now, with clearness, this :
What is with my bride amiss ?

In the evening fresh and bright,
Like a corpse she lies at night.

Naught has sounded, naught has stirred,
Ne'er a trace of breathing heard.

Filled with coldness is her frame,
E'en as if to dust it came."

" How can she be aught but dead,
Since her life but half is led ?

She dwells by day at home with thee,
At night her soul dwells in a tree.

Go to the stream beyond the park,
Thou find'st a willow with shining bark.

A yellow bough the tree doth bear,
The spirit of thy bride is there."

" I have not espoused my bride,
That with a willow she might abide.

Near to me my bride shall stay,
The willow in the earth decay."

In his arm the axe he held,
From the root the willow felled.

In the stream amain 'twas cast,
From the depths a murmur passed.

There came a murmur, there came a sigh,
As of a mother whose end is nigh.

As of a mother in death's embrace,
Who to her infant turns her face.

" Round my dwelling what a throng,
Wherefore sings the knell its song ? "

" The wife thou lovest is no more,
As by a sickle smitten sore.

At her toil she bore her well,
Till like a tree hewn down she fell.

And she sighed in death's embrace,
And to her infant turned her face."

" Ah, woe is me ! Ah, grievous woe ;
My bride, unwitting, I laid low.

In that same hour, thro' me was left
My child of mother's care bereft.

O thou willow, willow white,
Why did'st bring me to this plight ?

Half my life thou took'st from me ;
What shall I do unto thee ? "

" Let me from the stream be drawn,
And my yellow bough be sawn.

The wooden strips thou then shalt take,
And thereof a cradle make.

Lay the child therein to sleep,
That the poor mite may not weep

When he lies in slumber there,
He shall find his mother's care.

Plant the boughs by the water-side,
That no evil them betide.

Till he to a stripling grown,
Frame a reed-pipe for his own.

On the reed-pipe he will sing,
To his mother answering."

*The Garland* (1853).

JAN NERUDA

To My Mother

Know'st thou, dear mother, of the golden sun,
  And of his mother—legend passing fair,
Who, night by night upon her withered breast
  To slumber lulls her son far spent with care ?

Yea, the poor wight must rove enough, enough,
  Yea, all the day he thro' the world must go,
Enough grey mists and tempests, gloomy clouds,
  Almost as much as man bears here below.

A grey-beard he lies down, a youth he rises,
  With new-gained strength afresh o'er heaven
      he runs,—
O mother, mother, yea, thou righteous angel,—
  My need is e'en as grievous as the sun's.

                              *Book of Verses* (1867).

## SVATOPLUK ČECH

### Our Native Tongue

Power and fame and wealth—of all these things
    what doth to us remain ?
        Our native tongue.
What with a single shield did guard us in the
    wearisome campaign ?
        Our native tongue.

Let with a heavenly music sound, o'er half the
    world its mastery wield,
        A foreign tongue.
Queen of them all is in our eyes, and unto none
    the palm shall yield,
        Our native tongue.

And tho' it were a beggar-girl, and nothing but
    a maiden spurned—
        Our native tongue.
It is our will that it may to a glorious princess
    be turned—
        Our native tongue.

Be thou the apple of our eye, be thou to us more
    dear than all—
        Our native tongue.
And never thro' our failing care, upon it shall
    a shadow fall—
        Our native tongue.

There has no compact e'er been made, that can
    impose a price to pay
        On our native tongue.
Rather would we all surrender, than a jot should
    go astray
        From our native tongue.

Nay, ne'er shall be with our consent surrendered
    to an overlord,
        Our native tongue.
This sacred tongue's eternal rights shall ne'er by
    aught except the sword
        From us be wrung.

Ne'er shall it retreat, but ever farther onwards
    must it go—
        Our native tongue.
Ever higher must ascend, and ever more serenely
    glow—
        Our native tongue!

                    *New Songs* (1888).

## JAROSLAV VRCHLICKÝ

### Adagio

OVER the marble with its great drab shell,
 Where faded leaves in place of water lie,
The boughs of birches and of maples fell :
 All slumbers, save the scudding clouds on high.
Fain would I linger here in wistful poring,
 And gaze at evening drawing nigh this way ;
And at the hawk's gloom-covered, clamorous
  soaring,
 How o'er the wood he watches for his prey ;
Fain would I be this statue wrought in stone,
 On loneliness in forest-depths to brood,
Speaking with winds and echo all alone,
 Upon whose brow the night by day is wooed.

*A Year in the South* (1878).

JAROSLAV VRCHLICKÝ

Eclogue IV

SEE'ST thou how o'er the mountains morning is
        ablaze ?
Hear'st thou beneath the hedge-row how the
        grass-midge sings ?
O come to me : Theocritus has filled my heart
        with lays,
My soul is as a mead in rainbow colourings.
        What is it nigh my head doth sound ?
As though were flung a cymbal on the grassy
        ground.

Come, to the forest's marge amid the shade we fare,
The world shall see its image mirrowed in thine
        eyes,
O come and feast thy gaze upon the wine-gold
        air,
And on the dew that clad the buds in pearly guise,
        If, love, thou enviest the dower,
More than thou know'st, the fern upon thy locks
        will shower.

Or wouldst thou vale-wards go, and see the tints
        of red,
Decking the moss and leaves, and every ripening
        haw ?

Or art thou timid lest, ere thither we have sped,
Chance haply will avail, my lips to thine to
draw ?
Doth crimson on thy cheeks appear ?
A truce to berries, for thy lips are sweeter cheer !

Or shall we haply go together to the lake,
That 'neath the dusky leaves of water-flowers
is hid ?
Alder and willow-shades above the water shake,
The dragon-fly dips wings of amethyst amid
A fabled castle's crystal dome.
Thou, too, the Naiads' sister, findest there thy
home !

Or lov'st thou more the corn-field with its billowy
grain,
Where echoing melodies of flies and crickets
dart.
Thou rovest with thy musings o'er the grassy
plain,
Plucking, with joyous fingers, ear on ear apart.
Or wouldst thou in the clover-field,
Seek hours of joy, whose light is in thine eyes
revealed ?

Come, for the sun's first splendour on the country
falls,
His sheen is in thy heart, like to a thread of gold,
Entrust to him thy steps, and gain love's heavenly
halls,

Where youth doth to thy lips its draught of
    nectar hold.
    What is it nigh my head doth sound ?
As though were flung a cymbal on the grassy
    ground ?

*Eclogues and Songs* (1880).

## JAROSLAV VRCHLICKÝ

### The Grave-Yard in the Song

NIGHTINGALE, on whom in nights of splendour
    Hafiz was intent,
    Where sing'st thou now ?
Rose, o'er whom full often Dante, plunged in
    meditation, bent,
    Where bloom'st thou now ?
Star of sweetness, unto whose dream-laden bright-
    ness from his cell,
Tasso's woeful plaint was lifted and his thronging
    sighs were sent,
    Where gleam'st thou now ?
Heart, that out of flames wast woven, out of roses
    and of wine,

Heart of Sappho, whence by Eros lyric melodies
    were blent,
      Where beat'st thou now ?
Happy billow, that didst ripple tenderly round
    Hero's foot,
When Leander, faint from swimming, by the
    stormy waves was rent,
      Where flow'st thou now ?
Cast into the song your gaze, for there a mighty
    grave-yard lies,
'Neath whose surface all the bodies of the gods
    by man are pent,
      There weeps he now !

*Music in the Soul* (1886).

## JAROSLAV VRCHLICKÝ
### Melancholy Serenade XXII

NAUGHT brings such grievous pain,
As a flute with passionate strain,
  When in the rosy glow of eve
The gleams of daylight wane.

'Mid trees the murmurs flow,
In darkness lying low,
  Saying : " O ye dreams of youth,
Ye fill my soul with woe ! "

And it laments and sighs,
In tender, moving wise,
  As my belovèd, softly breathing
O'er my brow and eyes.

Hark ! the rushes render,
Accents dreamy, tender,
  And they quiver, as 'neath kisses
Thy bosom in its splendour.

They flow in sorrow blent.
Night is a flower ; there went
  From out its bosom, spreading langour,
A music-laden scent !

Naught brings such grievous pain
As a flute with passionate strain,
  When in the rosy glow of eve
The gleams of daylight wane.

*Music in the Soul* (1886).

## JAROSLAV VRCHLICKÝ

### Marco Polo

I, MARCO POLO, Christian and Venetian,
Acknowledge God the Trinity and cherish
Hope of salvation in eternity
For my sin-laden soul : In this my faith,
In this my trust is set. What of my love,
Ye ask ? And I give answer tranquilly :
My love is long and distant journeys ; ever
New-found horizons, new-found peoples, fresh
Exploits on ocean and dry land, and ever
Fresh enterprises. (This, my forebears' blood)
Much have I seen, to much have given ear ;
I reached the land, whereof ye scarce have inkling,
Where amber grows like golden foliage,
Where salamanders (that ye dub asbestos)
Blossom and blaze like lilies petrified,
Where glowing naphtha gushes from the earth,
Where there is equal wealth of rubies, as
Of holly here in winter ; where across
Their back and on their shoulders they tattoo
The image of an eagle ; where the women
Alone rule, and the men are given up
From birth to heavy service till they die.
I gazed upon the realm whose ruler is
Khan of Cathay ; and I have sat at meat
With those who feed on men : I was a wave

Amid the surf : the mighty emerald
(Pre-destined for the Vizier of Bagdad)
Beneath my tongue I carried through the desert.
For thirty days and nights I came not down
Out of my saddle. I have seen great deserts
Like ruffled raiment billowing afar ;
The ocean sleeping underneath the moon
Like a stiff winding-sheet ; strange stars ablaze
Beneath strange zones. I visited the realms
Of Prester John, where goodness, virtue and
Righteousness ruled, as in a legend,—yea,
Now meseems almost that I even reached
The wondrous nook of earth, where Alexander
Once lighted on the wilderness of Ind,
And came no farther on his way, because
Of mighty downpours that abated not.
(Perchance upon the faery realm he there
Set foot, or e'en upon the town celestial,
And shrank away in dread, when at the gate
An angel put a skull into his hand,
Saying : " A few more years, and this shall be
Thy portion,—this, and not a little more ! ")
And I beheld that land of mystery
Where lay the paradise of earth, where flowed
The spring of youth, concealed within the grass
Amid a thousand others, whence I drank
From many, and, 'tis very like, from youth :
And therefore all endured I with acclaim,
And therefore all, as in a mirror, I
Perceive within my soul, and now portray it.

The world is changed of aspect : I shall die
Like others, but my heritage remains.
The lust for seeing all and learning all,
To ransack all for the delight of man ;
Legion shall be my sons : they shall proceed
Farther than I, but scarcely shall see more,
For earth sheds wonders as a snake its skin.
Old age I know, with many dreams and secrets,
And that suffices me. And they who come
After me, let them take, as it may chance,
Of what remains to them, as best they can,
As I did. I sit foremost at the feast
Of distant journeys, and it likes me well,
All prospers me, and I fare well with all.
To make all life a vigil over books,
To rack one's brain 'mid piles of yellow parch-
     ments,
Seeking the truth of writing and of thought,
Is much, in sooth ; to live an age in camps
'Mid roll of drums and trumpets in assaults,
O'er ramparts in a rain of missiles, in
Ruins of towns, amid laments of women,
Weeping of children, groaning of the fallen,
Is much, in sooth ; to be a holy bishop,
Legions of spirits to escort to heaven
(The which he knoweth not) by solace of
The faith alone, and by the word of God,
In marble and in gold to hearken to
The cadence and the dreamy grief of psalms,
Is much, in sooth ; but to behold and know

With one's own eyes the distant, ample lands,
And oceans, plains and star-tracks of the skies,
And divers folk, their habit, usage, gods,
This too, availeth somewhat, and hath charm
By special token of its newness, that
Doth ever change.   And I have lived it through,
I, Marco Polo, Christian and Venetian.

*New Fragments of an Epic* (1894).


## ANTONÍN SOVA

### On the Hill-Side

HERE is the sweetest grass-plot for a bed,
    In softest lethargy to close the eyes,
On naught to brood, nor yearn, but let the head
    Droop in the grassy couch. . . . Like
        wreckage flies
A huddled clot of clouds, that yonder soar
    Behind the mountain's ridge. . . . All lulls
        thee here,
Insects adrone, grass, plant-stems bending o'er,
    The flight of sluggish moths. . . . To
        thee appear
Gleams as from waters, with a radiant leap.
    And by thy head there stands a calm unknown.
Thou feel'st 'tis wondrous with the dead to sleep,
    For Earth has cradle-ditties of her own !

*From my Country* (1893).

## ANTONÍN SOVA

### To Theodor Mommsen

To you, who have treacherously assailed my
    nation, covetous dotard,
Brutish, overweening!  To you, on the brink of
    the grave,
Arrogant bastard of Roman emperors and con-
    quering Germania ;
To you, dotard, blinded by vain-glory,
I chant the infuriate song of a barbarian, aroused
    by the smiting of hoofs.


With metallic buffetings
Scornfully I smite your enwrinkled visage,
O bestial fanatic of relentless Kaiserdom ;
Your shrivelled temples I smite, your turgid
    Neronic lips I smite,
Covered with foaming of impotent fury.


Was this the " reason " you discovered amid the
    ruins of Rome,
Which now seeks to lay in store of flesh for the
    slaughter-house,
And to shatter the brains of manacled and
    vanquished victims ?

For your unified Imperium to humiliate bonds-
    men in hordes,
Whom gladly you viewed trampled upon in
    triumphal arrays,
Humiliated by Roman Cæsars, the bondsmen in
    hordes,
Meet to be fashioned into saleable myrmidons to
    enrol for the Imperium.

Arrogant spokesman of slavery !
Do you behold naught else but the blossoming
    peaks of your country,
And all beyond would you leeringly crunch,
Beneath war-chariots of the conquerors
And their uncouth tread ?
Now, after battle-triumphs of your Imperium,
You hankered to enslave what of Europe
    remained,
To enslave, to enslave, woefully to enslave,
Bondsmen predestined for seizure, dung for
    enriching of soil,
Beasts to be yoked to the chariot of triumph
And from them you deemed barbarians, to break
    in levies.
For the Imperium, your insatiate Imperium.

But, even as once, long ago
We flouted the flabby wisdom of your Luther,
Reformer purveying peace unto contentedly
    fattened townsmen,

Begetting children with God-abiding spouses,
And stifling freedom,
So now do we flout your crude, senile wisdom !
It is enkindled not by sorrow for us, nor for all
    humanity ;
Therein is not the purity that perishes for its
    faith ;
Therein is not the passion wherewith the martyr
    of Constance* was ablaze ;
And therefore, brutish dotard,
Grown hoary in the service of your baneful
    Imperium,
From whose relentless wisdom are hidden the
    mysteries of maltreated spirits,
What avail you now your lore and your revered
    gray hairs ?
Your sorry wisdom has conceived not the light
    of righteousness,
Nor the gladness of youthful nations in their own
    destining ;
Has conceived not that an ancient culture durst
    not enslave,
Would it warm and illumine,
And not be but a chafing and burdensome
Monstrous millstone about the neck of a galley-
    slave !
What avail you revered gray hairs, since you babble
    senile saws,

* Hus.

O dotard, tottering on the brink of the grave ;
Since you have forgotten to proclaim unison and
    humaneness,
Destruction of tyrannies and of hatred ;
Since you have forgotten to reconcile your frail
    being with the world,
And to utter a prayer for all-accomplishing
    compassion ?
What avail you revered. gray hairs, since you
    drudge for darkness,
In an age when a myriad slaves hunger with an
    all-human suffering
And clamour at the portals of retrieval !
Since through the causeways of ancient cities
    range spirits of anarchy
Scoffing at your Kaiserdom ;
Since from down-trodden bondsmen of all castes
    and all nations,
Flicker the first torches of humanity,
Even as from amid the barbarians impaled upon
    stakes by Nero,
Blazed forth the lustre of Christendom !

Over your grave, that our grandsons shall forget
    not,
They will glitter, torches ablaze, unto your
    sightless eyes,
And will lay bare your words, wherein is sealed
    the downfall of your race ;
—But ere that, I, with the retaliation of disdain

Welling up from the sorrowful soil of this cowering
    age,
Advance to the rim of your grave,
And fling it upon you, despotical dotard,
That with this grinding reproach you may be
    burdened eternally, eternally  .  .  .

                        (1897).


ANTONÍN SOVA

Yellow Flowers

FIELDS of death grow sere in gloom,
Throbs the land with lute of doom.
Someone comes, a flower he strips,
Pressing it to feverish lips.

The agèd folk are on the brink,
And in sips their wine they drink.
On their locks the moonlight rests,
On withered skin and drooping breasts.

They will tarry yet a span,
Something yet their gaze will scan,—
Still to the fields they will not go,
Yellow blossoms rustle low.

They will not die.  They answer " No."

          *Sorrows Overcome* (1897).

## ANTONÍN SOVA

### Eternal Unrest

SPIRITED words had soaring zest,
The puny heart was frail and shy . . .
We can soar to each topmost crest,
Or linger here.  The heart sobbed : Try ! . . .
And when I made my endless heights my quest
The heart wailed here below despairingly . . .
And when with the heart I sank to rest,
The eagle's eyrie stirred me snaringly.

*Lyrics of Love and Life* (1907).

## ANTONÍN SOVA

O, That a Joy Might Come . . .

O, THAT a joy might come, calm, artless, marvelling . . .
Let us ponder and open the mire-bedaubed
windows,
The soul's festivity arises, morning-illumined
stillness.

Or that a joy might come, like evenings before a
festivity,
When blossoming trees amorously nestle towards
the moonlight,
And when cleansed thresholds beneath the stars
are aglimmer . . .

And the ample and free song-tune of Forgiveness
and Reconcilement,
O, that it might rove through all opened windows,
Through tumult of chimes, hosanna, hosanna
through the soul's festivity.

With wings uplifted, buoyant, shimmering, woven
of pliant fabrics
Of gold, carmine, of blue tinges from unknown
regions,—
O, that a joy might come, calm, artless, marvelling.

*Once again shall we return* (1900).

## ANTONÍN SOVA

### The Morning Wind

PLAYFULLY it arose above moist meadows
Beside living mountain-waters . . .
By cottages it dallied with bared heads of children,
Fair, curly-locked, winsome . . .
It fingered lilac and jasmine, roses and corn-ears,
Bespattered birds with dew, crinkled the grass
      upon tombs,
Unloosened ripples of fish-ponds in silvery
      cadences . . .

To be unleashed, unleashed, unleashed,
Was its smothered morning prayer . . .

Soon sated with play, idyllic and peaceful,
It dreamed of strength . . . To be unleashed,
      unleashed . . .
Amain to shrill through earth's miles, convoyed
      by swarthy clouds . . .
Dreamily to descend, asudden to dart upwards,
Above ridges of dark forests, where stags mourn-
      fully troat,
Even above murder in sequestered covert . . .

Was this then the self-same one, which, born early
      amid blossoms
Amid stillness of a fragrant valley,
Toyed with green tops of pine-trees

And passionately fondled tiny birds'-nests,—
Was this then the self-same one, which murdered
    at evening ?

Was this then the self-same one, which gently
    stroked tresses
And glowing faces, white and slender hands,
Whose fingers vied with it as they fluttered over
    piano-keys ?
Was this then the self-same one, which turmoiled
    at evening ?

Was this then the self-same one, at whose wafting
    halls were opened, thronging
With young bodies serried together,
Gardens freshly breathed, fragrance-laden, lamp-
    lights flickered
Swayingly upon sand-bestrewn pathways,
Weather-vanes sighed upon old towers,
And delicate music drifted through open balconies
    of green cottages ? . . .
Was this then the self-same one, which now
    ranted at nightfall ?

Behold : Wildly now it blusters in the stormy
    evening . . .
Has rended giant tree-trunks, flung nests to the
    earth,
Has trampled on clay hovels, with husky voice
    of horror
Has intoned an elemental song . . .

Assuredly it was the one   .   .   .   which, before
    gentle, refreshing,
Which seemed to seek strains of seraphic harps,
Murdered at evening   .   .   .
Gentle souls ! Gentle souls ! Gentlest souls !
Shall I remember that even ye, dreaming of your
    beauty and power,
One day will murder, frenziedly murder ?

*Morning and Evening Meditations* (1920).

## J. S. MACHAR

### October Sonnet

Only an anguished melody still flows
From earth where hazes spread a veiling net . . .
In every nook the faded beauty stows
Her faded blooms, lest springtime she forget.

But the desire, as ere to gladden, glows
Within ; unchilled her inmost ardour yet,
And gaudy sashes round her waist she throws
And asters in her tresses she has set.

Fain would she laugh as in her bygone days—
But 'mid her wrinkles laughter takes to flight
And from them only pity, pity cries . . .

Divining this, perchance she has surmise :
A hundred tears each morn her garb displays
Shed in the anguish of her sleepless night.

*Autumn Sonnets* (1892).

J. S. MACHAR

On Golgotha

IT was the third hour, when the cross was raised
Betwixt the crosses.
                        From their striving flushed
Upon the trampled, blood-stained earth, the
    soldiers
Had sat them down.  They shared the raiment
    out.
Then for the shirt, that had the woof throughout
They played at dice.
                        And many from the crowd
Approaching thither, turned their gazes upwards,
Wagging their heads, and jeering :  Ho, ho, ho,
Down from the cross,—'twas king you dubbed
    yourself !
You were the one, who would destroy the temple,
And in three days would build it up afresh,
Help now yourself !
                        Priests also tarried there,
And there were scribes with white and flowing
    beards ;
They said amongst themselves :  'Tis very true,
He would help others, let him help himself.
And from afar were many women gazing,
Who had of old served him in Galilee,

Salome, Mary and the Magdalene ;
They to Jerusalem had fared with him.
Numbered with rogues, he hung upon the cross,
Naked and shorn.   Upon his lash-seared body
Clung clots of blood.   And on his hands and feet
The red streak oozed, drops trickled to the earth.
With rigid stare his eyes were turned afar
Across the glittering town, the knolls and groves
To crests of peaceful hills, in whose lap lie
Blue waters of the Galilean lakes.

He bowed his head.
                    Then to his ear was wafted
The hum of plumage.   Not his Father's angel
With quickening draught for the exhausted soul,
An unclean spirit spread his vampire-wings
And scoured the air and lighted at his side.
He could not flinch, when Satan sat him down
Upon his cross,—yea, squatted at his head,
For his tired spirit was disarmed from strife.

And Satan said : " O hapless sufferer,
Upon this wooden cross we meet again,
To-day and then no more.   To-day 'tis settled,
The fight fought out.
                    You know, three years have passed,
Since in the wilderness I bore you forth
On to a lofty peak and let you see
Strong kingdoms, all the glory of the world,
And all I promised you, if you would sink

And kneel before me.  But you flouted it.
You went to preach the coming realm of heaven
Unto the poor, the weak.  To stainless hearts
You offered treasures of undwindling worth.
To simple souls you sought to show the way
Unto the Father's glory.  From men's brows
You strove to cleanse the trace of Adam's curse.
You turned to death with calm abandonment.
Like to the lamb, that opens not its mouth,
And you have shed your blood as it were dew,
So that your new-sown grain might not be
    parched.

Jesus of Nazareth, behold these throngs,
That surge like billows round about your cross!
'Tis not long since, when glorified you rode
Into the town, they littered palms beneath
Your ass-colt's hoofs, and they cried unto you
Your glory, and proclaimed you David's son,
For they supposed, that now the realm of God
Was heralded, and this the longed-for time
Of milk and honey.  But you flouted it.
The cozened throngs then in the wrath of
    vengeance
Dinned " Crucify ! " into the ears of Pilate.
And here they loiter, wagging with their heads
And jeering :    Yonder hangs the King of the
    Jews !
Find he his own help,—he's the Son of God.
His Father has, forsooth, forgotten him !

The Father has forgotten.

See this sky,
Where in full glory, you have deemed, he sits :
Cloudless and radiant it softly smiles
With that blue unimpassioned smile, the same
After you, as before you. And the birds,
Scouring the air, and every living creature
That roves the earth, has lived and lives to-day
After a single law,—and that is mine.
The stronger ever preys upon the weaker.
And so with mortals too. This whole wide world
Is my domain. For I am Life itself.
I rule alone. I lurk in hearts and souls,
And none shall hound me out or banish me.
Not you, and not your Father. Your God's
    Kingdom
Is dream. That dream I leave to men for ever.

Under the cross, behold the Roman captain
In peaceful converse with the white-haired
    scribe !
So shall it ever be. These twain inherit
Your words, your dreams. The one will change
    his idols,
The other his Jehovah in your name,
And in my covenant the world shall live.

Why did you scorn to take all kingdoms then,
And the world's glory from my bounteous hand ?
Then your young life would not have ended here

In shameful pangs, you might have lived un-
    trammelled
To your own gladness, to the weal of myriads.
What have you brought ? You sowed dispute
    and death,
Yourself first victim. For your name, your
    dreams,
Hundreds and hundreds yet will shed their blood
On crosses, in arenas, judgment-places.
And when it seems as though your dream has
    conquered,
Then in your name, and only in your name
Shall murder thrive. As far as eye shall see
Will stand a rank of flaring stakes, whereon
Burning of victims in your name shall be,
And in your name shall frenzied wars be waged,
And in your name shall towns be set ablaze,
And in your name shall countries be laid waste,
And in your name shall malediction speak,
And in your name shall there be servitude
Of body and of spirit.

                         See this captain
And here, this scribe. The first will, in your
    name,
Do murder and the second, in your name,
Will bless him. Millions of ill-fated men
Will forfeit for your dream their dearest portion,
Their life.

              And over all the squandered blood
Your dream of the eternal realm of God,

Of heavenly glory, will go drifting on
Like a mere wraith to recompense the dead,
To lure the living till the crack of doom !
Why did you scorn to take all kingdoms then
And glory of the earth ?   For mine is life,
I, I am life, and lord of all things here,
And age on age I lurk in hearts and souls ! "

And Satan then uprising, folded out
His tawny-hued and mighty vampire-wings,
Whose girth with stirring of a tempest waxed
Dread, overwhelming.  On all Golgotha,
Above the town, the valley and the hills,
Above the plain, above the distant mountains,
Above blue-watered lakes of Galilee,
Above the realms and oceans far-removed
The black and frowning mantle was outstretched.

And there was mighty gloom on all the earth,
And quaking.
                    And last time of all, the eyes
Of Jesus turned, and with loud voice he cried :
" Eloi, Eloi lama zabachtani ! "
And breathed away his spirit   .   .   .

Golgotha (1902).

## J. S. MACHAR

### Tractate on Patriotism

THAT nook of earth wherein I grew and lived
Through childhood, boyhood, and my years of
    youth
With all sweet folly of first love, with all
First pangs, deceit and misery of it ;
That one white township in the vale of Elbe
With dusky forests on the far horizon,
With its old castle, with its wild-grown park,
Its placid market-square, its church, that shaped
Outlandishly, peers forth with huddled tower
Across the country-side ; billowy fields ;
Avenued paths ; the agony of God
Where crossroads meet ; the meadow-lands that
    flank
Calm streams ; our cherished hamlets round
    about ;—
That nook of earth is all for which I crave
In the shrill streets of this afflicting city.
Yet rather is it craving for the years
Of youth I lived there. . . . Since the soul
    portrays
Fondly unto itself those places, craves
Piningly for them, while,—fond thing,—it
    harbours

A trembling hope that by returning thither
It may turn back its years of youth  .  .  .  I
    know
That I would likewise love another place
If I had passed elsewhere my years of youth. . .


This is my native land.  Naught else.  I lack
Aptness to worship that terrestrial
Concept, which diplomats have glibly framed
In their bureaus ;  which pedagogues to us
Imparted out of atlases ;  the which
Must needs, as each and all terrestrial
Concepts, to-morrow, maybe, shrivel or expand,
According as upon some battle-field,
In dreadful strife which is not our affair,
More striplings fall on that side or on this !


I have not found my pride in history,
That temple of idolators, wherein
Dreamers devoutly cast themselves to earth,
And in a frenzy beat their breasts because
They too are Czechs : nay, even as elsewhere,
Our annals are a file of dreadful deeds
(By us accomplished and by us endured)
Of recreant men, of surging passion-throes,
Betrayals, dominations and enslavements ;
And these befalling openly, became
Clear-ringing currency of daily catchwords
For tricksters of to-day, here as elsewhere.

Nor do I vaunt me of our own days.  We
Than others are no whit the better  .  .  .
We are but palterers and caitiffs ; where
Power is, there do we bend our necks to it
In slavish wise ; wherefore are we abased
By evil lords.  Time-serving braggarts we,
Testy and witless, laughing-stocks amid
Our pride, and palsied in vain peevishness.
Felons we have, dotards and pillagers
And hucksters dealing in pure love of country,
And a mere handful of the men who are
Ever untainted and downright,—but these
All nations have elsewhere,—ye gods, is this
To be, perchance, our fountain-head of pride ?

I am no patriot, nor do I love
My country, for I have none, know none, nor
See cause for loving one  .  .  .
I am a Czech, even as I might be
A German, Turk, Gypsy or negro, if
I had been born elsewhere.  My Czechdom is
The portion of my life which I do feel
Not as delight and bliss, but as a solemn
And inborn fealty.  My native land
Is within me alone ; and this will I
Trim round at no man's beck, nor give it tinge
To match with fashion's daily whim ; nor shall
They rob me of it ; when above my tomb
The grass has grown, it shall go living on
In other souls,—and if, some day to be,

In them it wither, then and only then
Shall it be lifeless, as old Kollár sang.

And if I toil for it, then that is toil
For Czechdom as I feel it in myself.

And if I ever pride me on it, then
I pride me only on my life  .  .  .

*Golgotha* (1902).

## J. S. MACHAR

### Shakespeare

Now gaze ye hither !
               Lo, a righteous judge
Set in the midst of monarchs, lords and knights,
Amorous women, raging termagants,
Mendicants, fools, placid philosophers,
Carousing artizans, hired soldiery,
Wizards and elfin sprites from fairy-land.

He laid bare the aching soul of them all,
Leaving it clear as crystal.  Of them all
He doth disclose the inmost consciences,
That he might show whereby in very sooth
Their deeds were prompted.
               Nor can bias hold
Sway over men before his countenance :

From the great king unto the mendicant,
Who drags his misery along the street,
All are but man.  He judges man, and passes
Sentence as unrelentingly as Fate ;
He has blood spilt, and it is naught but hazard,
If oft 'tis wont to be the blood of rank,
And royal blood sullied with sins.  For he
Can judge even a king, and sternly pass

Verdict upon him, and thereof is need
At sundry seasons.

                     Righteousness, the which
Is in the pay of this world's potentates,
By him is sentenced to the pillory.
From virtue, which has incense burnt before it,
The rose-hued mask he wrenches, and behold,
Abandoned strumpets, having each and all.
A death's-head, and the breathing of them reeks
With stenches of the tomb.  He punisheth
Evil which from out the human breast
Has thriven to a poisoned flower.  That too
He likewise punisheth, which guiltlessly
Is there entwined in the unshapen bud.

And from his judgment there is no appeal:
The heavens, the sun, the stars, the entire world—
These are but the beholders of his judgments.
And God ?  If such there be, then e'en God's
    judgment
Can be pronounced but by the lips of him.

*The Apostles* (1911).

J. S. MACHAR

Galileo with Milton at Torre Del Gallo

THIS tower they left me and the vault of heaven,
And so by day I gaze and gaze afar,
Into the world whereon I durst not step,
By night the starry ream, from whence I drew
Renown unto my name, grief for my life.
But threatens now relentless Destiny
To take e'en that.  My eyes are waxing weak,
And if I gaze without the helping lens,
I do but see a glimmering silvery dust.
You, Sire, are young, in life's heydey, a poet,
Son of the land which dragged its neck away
From grim and chilling clutches of the Church,—
O happy mortal. . . . Are we not myths to
    ourselves ?
At least I haply to you ?  I plainly showed
What before me Copernicus had found,
What e'en the sages taught in ancient Greece,
That this, our world, has no firm fundament
In starry space, but on predestined path
In a year's course rotates around the sun,
During the which, like a deft dancing-girl
Twists round its axis as it ranges on,—
And lo, then rose the Holy Church in wrath
And raged that I desired to shake belief

In truth of Holy Writ. Joshua, quoth 'a,
Spake once in war : Thou sun, shalt stay thy
    course
Up against Gibeon, whence 'tis passing clear
Itself must be twisting about our earth.
Ah, can you know, young man, what folly is ?
You know not, but I have quaffed it to the dregs,
When from their pulpits Jesuit Fathers spake
Homilies to the words of Holy Writ
As touching me : Why stand ye there, O men
Of Galilee and gaze aloft ? When they
Bade me deny the truth I e'en had spoken—
When unto Rome they summoned me to judgment
And they who judged are versed perchance in
    Scripture,
But never in those deathless, starry worlds,—
And when the Holy Father wroth thereat
(Not roused by mishap that befell the Scriptures
But deeming that I in my dialogue
I play the zany with his affirmations
And quiz him in a sorry figure which
Is called Simplicio in that same tractate)—
When at this long and never-ending trial,
I, sick and vexed by questionings and dicta
Whereat 'tis only possible to scoff—
When at this trial. I underwent perforce
Examen rigorosum, which is called
Torture in parlance of holy inquisition,—
(As though the deathless law can be o'erturned
When at the end a tortured human worm

Spake : Nay, it turneth not.  I spake thus ?
     Well,
I wot not)  Marvel not, O foreign sire,
At an old man, when he remembers, nay,
Remembers not, but clutches at his wounds,—
Wounds, quick and open :  that words, that
     phrases surge
Burstingly from his lips, so wild, pell-mell
E'en as thou heardest.  All in me is aquiver,
Voice upon lips, and blood in veins, and soul
In body,—yet the earth doth turn and turned
Aye, in spite of Joshua ; and it shall turn
Evermore, spite of Jesuits, and spite
Of Holy Inquisition  .  .  .  and herein
The myth of me  .  .  .
Gaze heavenward gaze,
Yonder, yea, yonder is the dayspring of
My earthly dolours all  .  .  .  in yon white
     lustres
Dayspring of all my woes, my prisoning
And earthly glory.  .  .  .  Weaker grows my
     gaze
Yon realm shall vanish from me soon.  .  .  .
     Perchance
Somewhere up yonder lies the solving of
That riddle which is dubbed the life of man.

                              *The Apostles* (1911).

## J. S. MACHAR

### Cromwell at the Corpse of Charles I

THE strength and soundness of this body promised
Long course of life.  .  .  .  Even as on King
     Saul,
The Lord bestowed all gifts on him, and him,
Even as Saul He sentenced with His sentence . . .
We were the voice of Him, the sword of Him.
He doth but lend authority to kings,
But gives the people power to judge a king ;
For kingly power thrives only from the people.
And since this Stuart was a murderer,
A traitor, tyrant, foe unto his people,
The spirit of the Lord departed from him,
And him His wrath delivered to our judgment.
Thus, after the exemplar of old times,
And as exemplar to all coming ages
Hath been this body's fate.  .  .  .  The people
     are
E'en as the apple of God's eye, and most
When the Lord yields a king unto their judgment.
Falsehood, deceit and feigning were his weapons,
And they are broken as a reed doth break ;
And all his men-at-arms and servitors
Bowed them like sheaves before our smiting
     swords.  .  .  .

Now staunchly onward, ever in God's counsel,
And from the earth blot we out all amongst us
Who in base pride run counter to the people—
And God thereof shall have his glory, and
A godly benison this land of ours.
Cherish we glowing trust upon the Lord,
And keep the powder in our muskets dry !

*The Apostles* (1911).


## PETR BEZRUČ

### Kyjov

Ho, ye youthful swains, top-booted and lithe,
   Ho, ye damsels in scarlet wear ;
In Kyjov town ye ever were blithe,
   And blithe shall ye ever be there.

E'en as from fragrant vines it had gushed,
   E'en as ye seethe, my lays ;
The blood of the Slovaks is fierily flushed,
   Lips burn and eyes are ablaze.

Who shall smite us, who shall afflict us with ill ?
   Of a master naught we know ;
And as blithe as we live and drink our fill,
   As blithe to our end we shall go.

*Silesian Songs* (1909).

## PETR BEZRUČ

### Ostrava

A HUNDRED years mutely I dwelt in the pit,
 A hundred years coal I hewed,
In a hundred years my shoulders were knit
 Stiff as if iron-thewed.

Coal-dust upon my eyes is smeared,
 The red from my lips has escaped,
And from my hair, from eyebrows, from beard,
 Coal clings icicle-shaped.

Bread with coal is my labour's prize,
 From toil unto toil I go.
Palaces by the Danube arise
 From my blood and my sweat they grow.

A hundred years I was mute in the mine,
 Who'll requite me those hundred years ?
When my hammer made them a threatening sign
 They each began with their jeers.

I should keep my wits, in the mine I should stay,
 For my masters still I should moil—
I swung the hammer,—blood flowed straightway
 On Polská Ostrava's soil.

All ye in Silesia, all ye, I say,
  Whether Peter your name be or Paul,
Your breasts ye must gird with steely array
  And thousands to battle must call;

All ye in Silesia, all ye, I say,
  Ye lords of the mines below;
The mines flare and reek, and there comes a day,
  A day when we'll take what we owe.

*Silesian Songs* (1909).

## PETR BEZRUČ

### I am the First of the Těšín People  . . .

I AM the first of the Těšín people,
First bard of the Bezkyds who uttered his strains.
Of the foreigner's plough and his mines they are
    bondsmen.
Watery, milky, the sap in their veins.
Each of them has a God in the heavens,
Greater the one in their native land.
In the church they pay him on high their tribute.
To the other with blood and a toil-seared hand.


He, he upon high, gave thee bread for thy life's
    sake,
Gave flowers to the butterfly, glades to the doe;
Thou, thou who were bred on the Bezkyd
    mountains,
To him the broad lands beneath Lysá dost owe.
He gave thee the mountains and gave thee the
    forests,
The fragrance borne by the breeze from the dale ;
At a swoop the other has taken all from thee,
Speed unto him in yon church, and wail.

Honour God and thy masters, my son from the
      Bezkyds,
And this shall yield fair fruit unto thee.
Thou art chased from thy forests by guardian
      angels,
So humbly to them thou bendest the knee :
" Thou thief from Krásná !   Is this thy timber ?
Thou shalt sink down meekly, and earth shalt
      thou kiss !
Quit thy lord's forests and get thee to Frýdek ! "
Thou upon high, what sayst thou to this ?

But thine ugly speech is a bane to thy masters,
To those guardian angels it is a bane,
Have done with it, thou shalt fare the better,
Thy son shall be first thereby to gain.
Thus it is.   The Lord wills it.   Night sank o'er
      my people,
We shall perish before the night be passed.
In this night, I have prayed to the Demon of
      Vengeance,
The first of the Bezkyd bards and the last.

*Silesian Songs* (1909).

## OTAKAR BŘEZINA

### Legend of Secret Guilt

Flash of my coming hours illumined this moment
in dreams
And bloomed in my festive halls with every lustre
ablaze,
My coming springtides and hidden graces rippled
in tuneful streams,
I was dazed by lips, with breath that beguiles,
with laughter that gleams,
And eyes where awaited me muteness of rapture
glowed there with yearning gaze.

But vainly I strode where quivered, in rhythms
that dumbfound,
Life's chant. The shadow of One before me and
after me wended,
Flitting from hall unto hall, bright blaze at its
coming was drowned.
Mirrors grew dim, yearning trembled and music's
conquering sound
As if thrust into lowliest octaves of silent anguish
was ended.

O my soul, whence came it ?   And how many
    centuries has it passed
Haply through souls of my forefathers, ere unto
    me it came ?
On how many marriage-tables as a requiem-cloth
    was it cast ?
On how many rose-hued smiles came its chill and
    earthen blast ?
And in how many lamps did it blanch amid salt
    and essence of flame ?

*Dawning of the West* (1896).

## OTAKAR BŘEZINA

### World of Plants

WORLD of plants.  Motionless the trees dream of
    their journeys
Through age-long change of guise.  Saps of earth
    blissfully trickled to them from darkness
And sweet to the sucklings was radiant milk of the
    sun.
And loftiest bliss : to set the delicate shape
Ablossom through secret of heaviness, and winds
    and lustre.  In depths blazes
Memory of fire.  Abundance from the overflowing
    cup and splendour of kisses
Are theme of fragrances' discourse.  Though all
    manner of insects may come,
Even them awaits here toil, and both the loathliest
And the loveliest are equally greeted by moon-
    pallor
And passionate flush of blossoms—O my soul,
    afar from us
Life flows here, plashing of a river which night has
    made remote.
Beneath silent stars I hear it murmur,
As in ferment it simmered through fire of tertiary
    ages.  In its mirror

Beheld morn and eve their colours' glory, secret
    reflex
Of eternal loveliness. Afar behind us it flows
    and rolls its depths to a sea
Whose tepid and blood-sweet waves bore us to
    these isles.
But stillness holds sway by the rocky springs and
    by shores of future earths,
And mute unto mortal hearing is the downfall
    of worlds
And likewise a new sun's first whirling in glooms
    of mystical night,
Even as fashioning of fragrance and thirst of the
    roots.

*Temple Builders* (1899).

## OTAKAR BŘEZINA

### Pure Morning

WHEN into the garden at morning-tide we entered
    weary with many dreams,
The whole of earth, like to our souls, we saw abloom
    in fiery gleams ;
And we to winds, to waters, plants, birds, bees a
    question sent :
What secret one this bygone night along our
    garden went ?

The sand, a golden changeling, lured where'er the
    sacred marks were shed
The waters murmured healingly, as set astir by
    angel tread,
Each breath had strength of life, as though for
    many glowing days,
And awe of new-engendered things was seen in
    every gaze.

Our grievous secrets' burden we as will of thine
    did not resist,
A missive that by humble lips, ere rending of the
    seal, is kissed ;
E'en at our gates the ambushed foe whom slumber
    overcame
As thine o'erwearied messenger we greeted with
    acclaim.

In havoc-ridden solitudes, that by the demon
    sprites are scoured,
As though it were a lily-bed, our cravings' tender
    garden flowered,
And women who most fervid were, most comely
    and most sweet,
As though our stainless sisters in their radiance
    we did greet.

*The Hands* (1901).

OTAKAR BŘEZINA

Responses

WE are curse-laden : even amid our yearnings'
loftiest flight
We by burden of earth are vanquished, plunged
into our blood's dim night—

" Ye are potent and deathless ; and in your
souls where secrets abound,
Suns and spring-tides and vintages numberless
are found."

In silence of cosmos, in midst of stars, that are
flecked with blood as they wane,
We are cut off in solitude, as by watch-fires of
foes in a chain.

" Armour of heavily-armed is your burden ;
unto contest ye
Are summoned, that ye therein may set all
earth-born creatures free."

Upon the riven breast of the vanquished we strive
to kneel,
And even when we yearn to love, no love we feel,
no love we feel.

" Hardened are ye like fruit, unripened ; but in
     the blaze
Of a secret summer ye ripen, your brethren's
     embraces to praise."

Gladness is sunshine beheld in a dream : on
     awakening it is dulled ;
Sorrow has thousands of eyes, and never in
     slumber is utterly lulled.

" With myriads in secret brotherhood ye are tied
And only in gladness of myriads will gladness of
     yours abide."

To floating islands upon a furrow of fragrance
     we float . . .
We float and the islands float onward, and keep us
     ever remote. . . .

" Blindfold are ye with deceit that your kingly
     glances wield :
Islands of radiance that bloom in your souls,
     before you they have revealed."

*The Hands* (1901).

### KAREL TOMAN

### Old Autumn Allegory

Leaves that the freakish craftsman's hammer
    thinned
From gold, bronze, tarnished copper, he flung
    away
Into the grass, a gift for children, for each wind.
    And dreamily watched their play.

In moonlit nights an old musician plies
Fiddle and flute by turns, for sheer delight ;
Playing for lovers' ears he seizes sobbing cries
    Of birds in southward flight.

And the compassionate poet, who could fuse
Betrayals', griefs', deceits' heart-crushing throes
To rhythmic dew and speech of crystal, comes to
    muse
    On calm that death bestows.

*The Sun-dial* (1913).

KAREL TOMAN

The Sun-dial

A HOUSE in ruins. On the crannied walls
  Moss gluttonously crawls
And lichens in a spongy rabble.

  The yard is rank with nettle-thickets
And toad-flax. In the poisoned water-pit
  Rats have a drinking-lair.
A sickly apple-tree, by lightning split,
  Knows not, if it bloomed e'er.

When days are clear, the whistling finches
Invade the rubble. Beaming, sunlit days
Liven the dial's arc that fronts the place,
And freakishly and gaily on its face
  Time's shadow dances
And to the sky recites in words of gloom :
  Sine sole nihil sum.
  For all is mask.

*The Sun-dial* (1913).

KAREL TOMAN

February

THOU who adorest peace and solitude
And amid depth of woods, and calm of snow-clad
    meadows
            Hearkenest to the beat of life,
            Dost thou not ever hear
            Voice of the depths ?

Far carnivals of slaughter, blood and death are
    heard,
            Earth's muteness is of woe.
            But below
The heart-beat stirs, and from the gloom a hidden
    well
            Thrusts itself lightwards.

        And tunes young waters chant
Quicken thy heart, and daze thy thoughts with
    joy that we
Though in despair, yet not alone in hope can be.

            *The Months* (1914-18).

KAREL TOMAN

April

A JOYOUS springtide shower of rain
And God's first rainbow o'er the countryside !
    The sower lays the seed-cloth down
        And trustfully
    Paces the soil where he has sown.

Though frosts may come, yet shall the sacred
    tilth
        Be never marred.
For its one statute is to burgeon and to thrive,
    To thrive though storm and sleet befall,
        Defying all.

The worthy grandsires warm them by the
    chimney-side
And ancient wisdom, ancient ways they ponder
    o'er,
        And ancient weather-lore.

                    *The Months* (1914-18).

## OTAKAR THEER
### Fire

O SACRED seething
In scarlet array.
Blossomed!  Flame-breathing!
Unto my heart with the fervid love-tinged
    utterance thrust thy way.
O scars, O weals,
How blissful are they that thy passion deals,
And what delight
From morn unto eve to be kindled and tested
By thy hundred tongues, branded, mauled,
    wrested,—
Yet with utter defiance to prevail amid evil plight.
Amid thy sacred forge may I never tire.
Like thy flames, and in thy dreaming's buoyant
    wise
Flash forth ever afresh, O my soul and with
    crimson wings press higher.
Out of each day shall a new redemption arise.
May at the last thine embrace, whither blood of
    the sun doth shower,
Snatch me in flight, O thou from the endless
    endlessly bursting power
Bear me and lay me to rest
Upon God's glowing breast.

*Anguish and Hope* (1912).

OTAKAR THEER

## Spake My Heart . . .

SPAKE my heart unto my will :
Why rackest thou me, that ne'er am still ?
Why snappest my growth ?  And my leafage
    wrest ?
Why marrest the song in each topmost nest ?

I desire to clutch dizzily sweet breath of spring,
I desire unto summer my branches to fling,
I desire to be fragrant, to lure, rustle, flower,
I desire a sun-gold, a star-silver dower.

Spake my will unto my heart :
It betides thee well, pampered thing that thou
    art !
Nearlong from bliss to bliss didst thou stray ;
But for me, thou wouldst know not sorrow nor
    sway.

Are we born for struggle, or born for dream ?
Are we water and vapour, or hill-top and gleam ?
I am mistress, thou'rt slave, hand am I, thing
    art thou,
At my bidding, as taper in tempest, to bow.

*In Spite of All* (1916).

## OTAKAR THEER

Drifting as in Dream He Dwells . . .

DRIFTING as in dream he dwells,
　Who with God has linked his powers.
　Through thy soul the span of hours
Bears its wizardry and spells.

Thou shalt fear nor dread nor dole
　As thou tread'st earth's meadow-land ;
　Thou art guided hand in hand
By God's wonder-working soul.

With this hand-clasp over thee,
　What is death and throes he wields ?
　Soul of God, through forests, fields,
Guide, protect, lead, foster me !

*In Spite of All* (1916).

### IVAN KRASKO

### The Slave

I AM he whose ears have heard the slave-mother
    singing her strains
Out of my soul this singing of hers never, never
    wanes.
With strange and stricken sorrow it sounded so
    forlorn
Across our plough-scarred landscape softly it was
    borne,
And seized upon the trembling spirit of a child.

I am he who beneath the lash of the task-master
    grew,
Beneath the lash that day by day opens unhealed
    wounds anew,
That never, never the trace of their weals can
    disappear.
Still my bended back cannot brace itself in its fear,
But a spark hidden till now gleams in my lowered
    gaze . . .

I am he who waits for the sound of the tocsin's
    boom,
That the slave who wreaks not vengeance shall go
    to a grievous doom.

When that I raise my back, and my face is set
    aglow.
Till then do I plant the trees, from which the
    gibbets grow  . . .
O, mournful it was to hear the slave-mother
    singing her strains !

*Verses* (1912).

IVAN KRASKO

Jehovah

CRUEL Jehovah! Thou who hast no pity,
Whose vengeance houndeth many generations,
Who hast destroyed the seed in the dry desert
Tainted by savour of foreign wont :
I plead to Thee for thine avenging hand,
Thy vengeance I call down on my own stock !
Let their mouths foam with long-continued
    wailing ;
Let unto task-masters be their greetings borne
By prayers wrung from their sickly, puny breasts ;
Let foreign fields be moistened with their sweat ;
Their backs lashed by the scourger, shall
Carry an irksome yoke throughout their lives ;
For ever let their craven hands
Implore for bread of their own toil ;
Their streams grow brackish to a searing gall,—
And let their loaves harden to granite blocks ;
Let their old men ne'er know what reverence is,
And let their offspring with a curse be laden ;
May'st thou drag love from out their women's
    hearts,
And in its place fill them with rancorous hatred ;
Let not the mothers bring forth poets among
    them

To cleanse their faces from the tears of blood ;
Let them perish deserted by the wayside,
And fetters be their music to the tomb ;
Let gibbets and no crosses deck their graveyards
And memory of them be ever shame :
If they will know not, that the hour is late,
That from a gloomy tower the tocsin rings.  .  .

.      .      .      .

Cruel Jehovah !  Who art pitiless,
I plead to Thee for thine avenging hand,
Thy vengeance I call down on my own stock !

*Nox  et  Solitudo* (1909).

# NOTE ON PRONUNCIATION

Czech vowels are pronounced distinctly as in Italian—no matter whether they are in stressed or unstressed syllables, whether they are long or short. Each vowel has only one pronunciation. Long vowels have diacritic signs (are accented) : *á, é, í, ú, ý*, short vowels are without diacritics (unaccented). Long *u* in the middle or at the end of words is marked with a little circle (ů). The dipthong *ou* sounds like the English *ou* in *soul*.

The diacritic sign (accent) on a vowel does not mean that the syllable is stressed. Long vowels occur very often in unstressed syllables.

The chief stress in Czech words is on the *first* syllable.

The consonants are pronounced as follows :

*c* like                    *ts* in *boots* (also in the group *ck*, e.g., *Palacký* [pà-la-tskee̅]).

*č* „                    *ch* in *chalk*.*

*ch* „    the Scottish *ch* in *loch*.

*dˇ* „                    *d* in *duty*.

*g* „                    *g* in *go* (occurs only in foreign and dialect words).

---

* *Cz* in the names *Czech, Czechoslovak* is pronounced like *č*, and so it is also spelt in Czech (*Čech, československý*). The spelling with *cz* is a concession to English printers.

*j* like         *y* in *you, boy.*

*ň* „           *n* in *I knew.*

*r* „ the Scottish *r* in *berry* (with the tip of the tongue).

*ř* approximately like the French *rj* if both consonants are pronounced at the same time.

*s* like        *s* in *son* (never like *z*).

*š* „          *sh* in *shilling.*

*tˇ* „ the first *t* in *tutor.*

*ž* „          *s* in *vision.*

Other consonants are pronounced approximately in the same way as in English.

*l* and *r*, being between two other consonants or after a consonant at the end of a word, have the value of a vowel, e.g., in the names *Vltava* [vl̀-tă-vă], *Vrchlický* [vr̩ch-li-tskee̅], *Brno* [br̩-nŏ], *Přemysl* [přè-mÿ-sl̩].

*d, t, n* before *i, í,* or *ě* are pronounced like *dˇ, tˇ, ň.* After other consonants *ě* is pronounced like *ye* in *yes*, e.g., *běs* [byes] = demon, *pěšina* [pyèshïnă] = foot-path, *věda* [vyèda] = science.

# BIBLIOGRAPHY

Císař, J.—Pokorný, F. : The Czechoslovak
Republic. A Survey of its History and
Geography, its Political and Cultural
Organisation, and its Economic Resources.
With numerous illustrations and a map.
T. Fisher Unwin, London, 1922.

Czech Folk Tales. Selected and Translated
by Dr. Josef Baudiš. With eight
illustrations. George Allen & Unwin,
London, 1917.

Čapek, Karel. R.U.R. Authorised translation
by P. Selver. London, Oxford University Press. New York, Doubleday
Page, 1922.

Denis, Ernest : Huss et la guerre des Hussites.
E. Leroux, Paris, 1878.

Fin de l'Indépendence bohême. 2 vols.
A. Colin & Cie, Paris, 1890.

La Bohême depuis la Montagne-Blanche.
2 vols. E. Leroux, Paris, 1903.

Les Slovaques. Delagrave, Paris, 1917.

Eisenmann, Louis : La Tchécoslovaquie. (Les
états contemporains). F. Rieder & Cie,
Paris, 1921.

GRAHAM, STEPHEN : Europe—Whither Bound ?
(Quo Vadis Europa ?)  Being letters of
travel from the capitals of Europe in the
year 1921.  (Chapter IX and passim.)
Thornton Butterworth, London, 1922.

KOMENSKÝ, J. A. : The Labyrinth of the World
and the Paradise of the Heart.  Edited
and Englished by the Count Lützow.
Second edition.  (The Temple Classics.)
J. M. Dent & Co., London, 1905.

LÜTZOW, COUNT FRANCIS : Bohemia.  An
Historical  Sketch.  Third  edition.
(Everyman's  Library.)  J. M. Dent &
Sons, London, 1920.

A History of Bohemian Literature.  Second
edition.  W. Heinemann, London, 1907.

Lectures on the Historians of Bohemia.  Being
Ilchester  lectures  for  the  year  1904.
Henry Frowde, London, 1905.

The Story of Prague.  Third edition.  J. M.
Dent & Sons, London, 1920.

Life and Times of Master John Hus.  Second
edition.  J. M. Dent & Sons, London,
1921.

The Hussite Wars.  J. M. Dent & Sons,
London, 1914.

MACHAR, J. S. : The Jail. Experiences in 1916. Authorised translation from the Czech by P. Selver. Basil Blackwell, Oxford, 1921.

MASARYK, T. G. : L'Europe Nouvelle. Imprimerie slave. Paris, 1918. [The English edition, under the title " The New Europe. (The Slav Standpoint)," was printed in London, 1918, for private circulation only.]

The Spirit of Russia : Studies in History, Literature and Philosophy. 2 vols. Translated by E. & C. Paul. George Allen & Unwin, 1919.

MAURICE, C. EDMUND : Bohemia : from the Earliest Times to the Foundation of the Czechoslovak Republic. Second edition. T. Fisher Unwin, London, 1922.

NOSEK, VLADIMÍR : Independent Bohemia. An account of the Czechoslovak Struggle for Liberty. J. M. Dent & Sons, London, 1918.

NOVÁK, ARNE : Czech Literature during and after the War. (" The Slavonic Review," No. 4, June, 1923.)

SCOTUS VIATOR (R. W. Seton-Watson) : Racial Problems in Hungary. Constable & Co., London, 1908.

SELVER, PAUL : Anthology of Modern Bohemian Poetry. Drane, London, 1912.

Anthology of Modern Slavonic Literature, in Prose and Verse. Kegan Paul, Trench, Trubner & Co., London, 1919.

Modern Czech Poetry. Selected Texts with Translations and an Introduction. Kegan Paul, Trench, Trubner & Co., London, 1920.

Otakar Březina. A Study in Czech Literature. Basil Blackwell, Oxford, 1921.

SETON-WATSON, R. W.: German, Slav and Magyar. Williams & Norgate, London, 1916.

Europe in the Melting-Pot. Macmillan & Co., London, 1919.

# INDEX

Aleš, M., 6, 79, 149, 151
*Alexandreis,* 13-14
Amazons, Czech, 5
Arany, J., 123, 143
Archives of the Bohemian Brethren, 45-46
Ariosto, L., 122
Augusta, Jan, 44
Austrian absolutism, 103, 105, 114
Austrian Constitution of 1848, 97

Bach, Austrian Minister, 103, 114
Balbín, Bohuslav, 60-61
Bâle, General Council of, 28
Bartoš Písař, 44-45, 91
Baudelaire, C., 122
Baudiš, J., 273
Bendl, K., 136
Bernolák, A., 112
Bethlehem Chapel, in Prague, 26, 28
Bezruč, Petr, 159-161, 246-250
Bible of Kralice, 47, 112
Bílek, Jakub, 43-44
Bivoj, 5
Blahoslav, Jan, 46-47
*Book of Rožmberk,* 16
Bořivoj, Prince of Bohemia, 6
Bowring, John, 69
Brethren, The Bohemian and Moravian, 39, 40, 41.
Brethren of Chelčice, The, 38
Břevnov, Monastery of, 15
Březina, Otakar, 123, 151, 168-175, 251-258, 276
Brixen, in the Tyrol, 103
Budovec, Václav, of Budov, 51
Burns, Robert, 127
Byron, Lord, 108, 115, 118, 122, 132, 137

Calderon, 122
Camoëns, Luiz, 122
Čapek, Karel, 176, 273
Carducci, G., 122

*Časopis Musea Království českého,* 97
Catherine, St., The Legend of, 20
Čech, Svatopluk, 131-134, 138, 177, 207
Čechy (= Bohemia), 4.
Čelakovský, F. L., 88-90, 106
*Česká Včela,* 102
Charles IV, King of Bohemia, 8, 17, 18-19, 21, 144
Chelčický, Petr, 24, 33-38, 175, 185
Chocholoušek, P., 134
Christian, monk, 9
Church Reform, 19, 23, 24, 26, 28, 31
Císař, J., 273
Coleridge, S. T., 127
Comenius, *see* Komenský
Constance, General Council of, 27, 28
Constantine (Cyril), 6, 7, 10
Constantine, Roman Emperor, 35
Coppée, F., 162, 163
Cosmas of Prague, 3, 9-10, 20
Critical movement, in the eighties and nineties, 145, 149

Dalimil, 14
Dante, 85, 122
Decadents, The, 130, 161
*Decalogue, The,* 16
Decree of Tolerance, 64
Denis, E., 273
Didactic poems, 16
Dobner, Gelasius, 67-68, 92
Dobrovský, Josef, 67, 68-71, 75, 76, 77, 92, 95
Dorothy, St., The Legend of, 20
Dostoyevsky, F. M., 152
Durych, Václav Fortunát, 68
Dvořák, A., 144

Eisenmann, Louis, 273
Eliška Přemyslovna, 6, 17
Engels, F., 146
Erben, K. J., 88, 90-92, 200